TIM

the PLAN B PRAYER

LIVING *with the* LOSS *of the* IDEAL

First published in 2015 by Striving Together Publications, a ministry of Lancaster Baptist Church, Lancaster, CA 93535. Striving Together Publications is committed to providing tried, trusted, and proven books that will further equip local churches to carry out the Great Commission. Your comments and suggestions are valued.

Striving Together Publications
4020 E. Lancaster Blvd.
Lancaster, CA 93535
800.201.7748

Cover design by Andrew Jones
Layout by Craig Parker
Special thanks to our proofreaders

The author and publication team have put forth every effort to give proper credit to quotes and thoughts that are not original with the author. It is not our intent to claim originality with any quote or thought that could not readily be tied to an original source.

ISBN 978-1-59894-290-3

Printed in the United States of America

DEDICATION

This book is dedicated to my children Matthew, Michael, McKayla and Mark. I love my kids. They love me. It is my prayer that I can leave behind a legacy of faith for them through the pages of this book.

One of the incredible aspects of God's Word is the transparent exposure of human emotion and experience. Psalm 90, the only psalm penned by Moses, is such a passage. In these seventeen verses, we hear the heartfelt cry of a man who found himself on a path different than he expected. And in *The Plan B Prayer,* we hear these truths echoed through the pen of another who has personally applied them to his life. In this insightful study of Psalm 90, Pastor Tim Zacharias transparently shares experiences from his life that have given him personal understanding of what it means to walk through difficult times. In these pages, you'll find encouragement and application that will strengthen your hope and deepen your understanding of God.

—Dr. Paul Chappell, Pastor of Lancaster Baptist Church and President of West Coast Baptist College, Lancaster, California

Psalm 90 comes alive as never before in the marvelously written book by Pastor Zacharias. It is biblical, practical and well thought out. For those of us, like Pastor Zacharias, who are living with a medical "sentence of death," this book gives us a reason to live above the circumstances in which we find ourselves. I highly recommend it to everyone, for we are either entering a storm, in the midst of a storm, or coming out of a storm. *The Plan B Prayer* is a must read for every pastor and a great tool for helping those in their darkest hours!

—Dr. Earl Jessup, President and Founder of Baptist Church Planting Ministry, Ontario, Canada

Pastor Tim Zacharias' clear, succinct, and structured verse-by-verse analysis of Moses' prayerful response to the divine chastening of being forbidden from entering the Promised Land will be a blessing to any truth-seeking Christian who is struggling in the face of the trials of life.

—Nathaniel Khng, Yale Law School Graduate and Attorney, Singapore

The Plan B Prayer is doctrinally sound, faithful, and clear in interpretation of Scripture. It is written with the compassion and understanding of a man who has learned at the feet of Jesus. Those who are walking a similar path as Moses will find this book both instructive and comforting. Surely all of God's children who are serious in their relationship with Him must confront the issue of failure or redirection at some point in life. You will find in this book the teaching and encouragement that you need.

—Dr. Joel Mullenix, Vice President of Pensacola Christian College, Pensacola, Florida

Pastor Zacharias journeys transparently through Psalm 90 with profound personal insight and life-changing perspective. This book will deepen your hope in God's eternal purposes and strengthen your faith through hardship. Every chapter is rich with scriptural truth and personal application that will anchor you to God's unchanging heart in spite of the uncertainties of our temporal world.

—Cary Schmidt, Pastor of Emmanuel Baptist Church, Newington, Connecticut

CONTENTS

INTRODUCTION

CANAAN LOST

What do you do when you miss the mark and the ideal is lost?

What do you do when you realize that the perfect plan will never happen?

What do you do when the plush plains of the Promised Land become increasingly out of sight?

Moses was in this situation. How did he think? What did he do?

He prayed the "Plan B" prayer!

Canaan...

For the sincere Bible believer, the name conjures up pleasant images. It was "a land flowing with milk and honey" (Exodus 3:8). Every commentator takes an educated guess as to what that means. It could be a proverbial expression as in "a land of abundance." The description might be a more literal rendering, speaking of the fact that Canaan would be a good land to pasture cows—a land full of foliage and flowers needed for honeybees to make their sweet dessert. I don't know exactly myself, but whatever it means, it sounds good. For the nation of Israel, this was the land of promise. And God described it in such a way as to convey that it had everything they could possibly need and want. Who would not have wanted to live in Canaan?

Some of our traditional Christian hymns relate Canaan to Heaven. Crossing Jordan is equated with dying, and the Promised Land of Canaan is our place of final rest. Heaven, like Canaan, is Beulah land.

Is this analogy true to form? I don't think so. There may be some slight symbolic relationship between Canaan and Heaven, but the parallel falls short in that Canaan was a place of conflict. Israel had to fight for the Promised Land. Eventually they were expelled from it because of their disobedience. These things are not true of Heaven. There is no conflict or sin in Heaven. And, thank God, no one is given the boot.

Also, if Canaan relates to Heaven, then how does the wilderness wandering relate to the Christian experience? It would seem, if the type were true, that the whole Christian experience would be one of rambling, digression, and defeat.

Hebrews 3:14–19 and 4:4–10 speak of a correlation between Canaan and the present Christian experience. This is a general reference for sure. It simply says that we have a rest today, just as was promised to Israel in Canaan. We cease from our works for salvation from sin and rest in the finished work of Jesus on the cross. We must be careful not to stretch the application farther than that point—at least not from this passage.

In 1 Corinthians 10:1–11 we find another practical application for believers today relating to the trek to Canaan. It is conveyed in negative terms only. This passage repeats the fact that many of the children of Israel did not enter into the place of promise. They lusted after evil things. They looked back to Egypt with longing. They demanded God's blessing and complained when God did not respond or when He disciplined them. Ultimately, they stood paralyzed at the threshold of the Promised Land and rejected entrance due to unbelief. Victory was theirs. Rest was waiting for them; yet, they would not believe that God could provide such privilege. They did not exercise the courage necessary to make a move.

The positive inference from this passage is that Canaan represents the abundant, victorious Christian life. Therefore, the illustration of Canaan applies to us as New Testament believers, not only in our initial confidence in the redemptive work of Christ, but also in our ongoing faith in all of the promises related to our life in Christ. God has given us a Book full of great and precious promises that must be appropriated by faith. Either we believe them and act accordingly, or we do not.

As we read the account of Israel's wilderness wandering, we see an illustration of people in our modern ranks—Christians with boundless potential in Christ but resigned to live a trudging life of survival because of resistance to God and unbelief. Canaan is lost to them. The land flowing with milk and honey is in view, but they never cross the border and confidently take their ground; they never fully find their place of privilege.

In the Bible account, a generation not only missed out on Canaan but also lived and died in the desert. This is a sad image to behold. It is this picture that demands our strongest consideration. We must aspire to the path of faith and reject the temptation to doubt God and deny that which He has promised. This is the moral of the story in what it represents to us today.

Yet, there is a more personal illustration and image in the record that holds its own unique application. What about Moses? How does the experience of Moses relate to us?

Moses was not consigned to the wilderness because of disbelief in God. Not only did he believe that God could provide the Promised Land, but also, he forfeited all he possessed to see it happen. Moses faced danger and accepted the daunting task of leading God's people to venture towards the land of promise, but Canaan was lost to him as well. Why?

Moses was required to lead an unfaithful people back into the wilderness for forty more years. This was a circumstance beyond his control. God's punishment for the Israelites' disbelief (a disbelief Moses did not share) would be that a generation of Jews would die in the desert. Only a faithful few and the younger generation would live and take possession of Canaan. Moses would be one of those to take the Promised

Land in time. Yet, his detour turned into a dead end because of one act of disobedience—one false move, that's all.

You know the fateful facts. Moses was instructed by God to speak to a rock that would provide a miraculous supply of water for the thirsty throng of demanding and murmuring Israelites. Instead, in anger towards the people, he struck the rock (Numbers 20:6–11). His frustration seemed justifiable. His deviation from God's command seemed somewhat minor. (Of course, there is no such thing as minor disobedience, but some sins are not as serious as others in relation to earthly consequence.) For his error, God said that Moses could not enter Canaan.

Anyone with any shred of empathy would feel sorry for Moses. Was it really worth such a serious consequence? Why did God have to be so harsh?

The main reason cited by God was that Moses did not "sanctify" Him in the eyes of the people (Numbers 20:12). In other words, he did not set God apart as the Sovereign Authority. He directly disobeyed God in front of everyone.

Moses was the mediator of the Law, and as such, God held him to a higher standard. Moses represented the exactness of God's moral standard to the people. One public display of direct disobedience was enough to cause him to remain with the multitude of malcontents in the uninhabited outskirts of Canaan.

Oooh, that hurts!

For Moses, this experience represented the death of a dream—the loss of an ideal. This was more than hope deferred; this was hope denied. Moses knew what it meant to miss out on the full measure of God's perfect will.

Maybe you do as well.

It breaks your heart when the blessings that you've envisioned for your life are hopelessly lost.

It could be that, like Moses, an unexpected trial of faith beyond your control has taken you on a circuitous route on which you never thought you would travel. It may be, as with Moses again, that you have sinned and set in motion a series of consequences and circumstances that have changed the course of your life. Things are different now than they could have been. Your movements in life have been modified. Your direction is different now, and your aspirations must be altered. That is what this book is all about.

To understand the premise presented within these pages, you must put out of your mind the typical thoughts about Canaan. You must not see Canaan as Heaven or the victorious Christian life. You must see Canaan in real time as you look through the eyes of Moses. To him, Canaan represented an unrealized ideal condition or an unreached goal in God's perfect will.

This book is about how to experience blessing when the beautified condition you once imagined for your life is out of reach.

Moses wrote a scriptural psalm about this topic. He penned Psalm 90 after his exit on the road to Canaan. It reads like no other psalm. Its subject matter is unique. Its poetic cadence is different. It has an air of both disappointment and promise.

This psalm has a special place in my heart not only because I can relate to its message, but also because it was one of the first passages I chose to preach from at the inception of our newly-planted church in Connecticut. I preached a sermon from verses 14–17 entitled "A Vision of Blessing."

In my personal devotional life, I find myself going back to Psalm 90 again and again to deal with the ideal images that have been marred in my life. I find in these words profound principles that help me find blessing in situations which I would otherwise discount as misfortune and blight.

I hesitate to repeat each adverse account of tribulation in my life. My last book, *Working Through an Asaph Moment* tells it all. I will limit my rehearsal to a quick summary.

My wife, Stacie, and I entered into marriage and the ministry with glorious imaginations. We soon experienced trials beyond our wildest conceptions. Over a process of thirteen years, Stacie endured seven miscarriages. It looked as if we would never have children.

We lowered our expectations for natural birth, and what was once a dream had to be relegated to a nagging interest. Then we turned our hope in another direction as we began to look into adoption. It seemed like a miracle when God connected us with an available four-year-old boy with special needs. The dream was still alive. And yet, in the end, what started with such promise became, in time, the greatest trial of affliction.

Our son had more problems than we could handle. At age thirteen, we had to send him to a therapeutic facility and program. For the rest of his teenage years he basically moved from one program to another until he was old enough to be on his own. This is not what we had envisioned for him or us.

Some days it seemed as if a dark cloud was over our heads. Almost every day was filled with the conflict at hand. In our few quiet moments, we would ask ourselves, and God, "What happened, and how did we get here?" As we still endure the effects of this long trial, we can most assuredly relate with Moses as the picturesque plan for his life was altered by the actions of those around him.

This was only one aspect of our lives that did not go as planned. We adopted another special needs son. He came to us with developmental delays, and the challenges of rearing him were far greater than we had imagined.

As the years passed and as older adults, God eventually gave us two biological babies. This was much to our surprise and the doctors' dismay. Maybe we were too idealistic at first, but our family was being formed in a fashion we could not have conceived. It's not that our dreams died completely; they just took on a different composition.

The ministry was not exactly what we thought it would be either. It's hard to go into a work with eyes wide opened when you don't really know what you are looking for.

At first, I guess we expected much more cooperation from the young people and parents we were called to serve. I was a young youth pastor with big plans. I did not anticipate the serious, spiritual struggles involved in snatching souls from the fire and guiding young Christian pilgrims on the narrow way. Don't get me wrong; I was blessed beyond measure to have the privilege to serve the Lord in this way. It was just not as picture-perfect as I had hoped.

In time and through a process of amazing circumstances, God moved in our hearts to plant a church in the Northeast—a new place with new promise. This time our eyes were opened—wide enough to know that we were in for a challenge but not wide enough to see what exactly that challenge would be.

In our weak moments we may think, "This is more than we bargained for." But God is good. He gives us enough blessings to keep us going. His mercies are new every day.

Stacie and I have a lot for which to be thankful. What started with empty seats in a conference room of a hotel has now developed into a thriving church family. We love our church family. It is strong, loving, healthy, and alive. A Bible-believing congregation has been firmly planted in a traditional New England town. Every day we are amazed at all God has done.

Through it all we have come to learn that our expectations must be based on the real conditions of the moment, not some illusory view of better days. Some of our complications have come from conditions beyond our control. Some are from decisions of our own choosing. In the process of time, we have learned that there is no better day than today. Today is all we have. We still look ahead with longing but avoid the temptation to form firm determinations of what life must be.

Four years ago, I was diagnosed with cancer. I have Multiple Myeloma—a terminal and incurable disease. Thank God, my cancer is treatable to some extent. Thank God for His mercy to answer prayer and extend my life and ministry.

As I begin writing this book, I am four years into remission after a stem cell transplant. The doctors say that for a person my age, a stem cell transplant is usually effective for three-to-five years. In my weak moments, this weighs heavily on my mind. If I let it, this wary thought will paralyze me.

I always thought that cancer was for other people. It could never happen to me. Don't we all, to some degree, live with the deluded notion that we are invincible? For me, this condition has reinforced the fact that my future on earth cannot be manufactured in my mind. I must face what is before me. Only the Lord can help me do that.

As He was doing with Moses by leading him back into the desert, I think that God was using my disease to discipline me. He is purging me, and at the same time, preparing me for different avenues of ministry. I find Psalm 90 to be a paradigm for my prayers of blessing in the midst of life's trials. The inspired words of Moses are instructive as he prays to God for blessing in the midst of hardship.

In these pages, we will look at the bare words of Psalm 90 and draw conclusions that are upfront and clear. We will follow the progression of the principles contained in the psalm and let the truth of it take us where it will.

Each chapter begins with a short section of the psalm forming a focused, contextual framework. At the end of each chapter is a study section leading to diverse and yet parallel places. The format is intended to make it useful not only for personal reading but also for group Bible study.

In this journey together, we will find that whenever God redirects, He always leads to a place where blessings are formed in fashion with new experiences—maybe not the ones we saw coming but divinely designed and ultimately good nonetheless.

My prayer is that as you read, you will relish the journey and learn to embrace whatever road God has for you to take.

CHAPTER ONE

A PRAYER OF MOSES, THE MAN OF GOD

We should not be surprised that Moses wrote a psalm, for he was both a prophet and a poet.

One of his songs is recorded in Exodus 15:1–19. It is written in repetitive-verse form and was so lyrical and lively that Miriam joined in leading other women in timbrel and dance (Exodus 15:20, 21).

A longer song of Moses is recited in Deuteronomy 32:1–43. This song was spoken as a poetic recollection of God's work in the world and among the nation of Israel. Joshua helped Moses pronounce this prose to the people. Without the aid of microphones and amplified sound, together their voices somehow teamed together to reach the ears of the multitude of Israel.

Psalm 90 is just one selection in Moses' personal psaltery. It reads like a prayer as it is spoken directly to God.

Moses was a man of close fellowship with God. He was called a "man of God," "servant of God," and, more intimately, the man "whom the Lord knew face to face" (Deuteronomy 33:1 and 34:10). How much closer to God can you get?

Only a man with these unique credentials could write a psalm like Psalm 90.

In these verses, Moses speaks of God and to God in such a way that could only be possible by a depth of discovery most Christians don't care to reach. It is possible that he knew God more intimately than anyone in history. This true man of God was able to write a prayerful psalm with transcendent tones and transparency of soul.

God and Moses had been through a lot together. As God was preparing Moses to lead His covenant people, He led him through a series of extremes. To be ready for his mission, Moses had to take a long trip on the rolling hills of the abounding and abasing thoroughfare.

Moses started out the son of a slave and soon became the adopted son of the Pharaoh of Egypt's daughter. After forty years of being groomed for royalty in the courts and palaces, he left it all to be identified with his true people—the Israelites, the slave society of Egypt. He went from great wealth to great deprivation. After a brazen display of loyalty to his people, he was forced to flee Egypt.

Driven from his homeland, Moses found a place to reside in the sandy settlement of Midian. This man who was a leader of men now became a keeper of sheep—yes, sheep—you know, those dirty, loud and stubborn creatures that run the ragged countryside. Sounds like good training for leading a stubborn multitude of men, women, and children through a desert. Moses did not know it at the time, but he was being conditioned and qualified to lead God's people, the Jews, from Egypt to the Promised Land. Midian was God's training ground for what was coming—a cause and a quest to chart a course towards Canaan.

In Egypt, the nation of Israel had been living in slavery for over four long centuries. They needed a deliverer. They longed for a hero, and God had determined that Moses was the man for the job. God was with Moses and endowed him with supernatural power to plague the Egyptians until the Pharaoh had no other recourse but to let the Israelites go.

Moses led the people through the Red Sea. He took them through the wilderness and to the edge of Canaan. This was the culmination of his calling. This was the destination that he had dreamed of ever since leaving Midian. This was the cause for which he risked it all. This was it! This was everything!

This was the Promised Land!

Can you imagine his frustration when at the point of entry, the people refused to believe God's promises and enter in? Because of their unbelief, God sent them back into the wilderness to die. Only their children as well as the faithful and believing few would be allowed to survive and enter. It would take forty more years for that to happen.

It is hard to say one way or the other, but it seems as if Psalm 90 was written either at the onset of the wilderness wandering, or at the end of it.

In verse 10, Moses states that the average human life is seventy years—eighty at the most. This verse suggests that this psalm was written early on. Moses was near eighty when the wilderness wandering began. He may have been writing this prayer about preparing a generation to go into Canaan believing that he was living on borrowed time.

The prayer for early satisfaction in verse 14 also clues the reader to the timing of the psalm. It seems to speak of the commencement of the wilderness journey.

The only aspect of the psalm that may give us pause to assume an early date is the fact that verse 15 speaks of affliction in the past tense—as if Moses and the people had already endured much tribulation. They had seen "evil" for "years."

If Moses wrote this later in the wilderness experience, the psalm would seem to fit the theme of what Moses might have been thinking when he learned that he would have to go back into the wilderness after his own sin. The tenor is such that it suggests Moses knew that he would never possess Canaan personally. Not until the end did he know that fact. To me, this is the most viable understanding of the text. My exposition here begins with that assumption.

No matter which position you take as to the timing of the psalm, the overall theme is the same. At the time Moses penned the psalm he was deprived of Canaan. He was missing out on a grand experience in the perfect will of God. He was praying that God would give him grace to deal with the complications of living with Plan B.

There is one verse in the Bible that states that there is such an experience as "the perfect will of God." It is Romans 12:2. This verse says that by the renewing of our minds, we may "prove what is that good, and acceptable, and perfect, will of God."

The renewing of our minds refers to the change in thinking that comes from a constant confrontation with God's revelation—His Word. Since the completion of God's written revelation, and in our present relational economy with God, it is the Bible that helps us to live in conjunction with God's will.

At this point, it is important to distinguish that in speaking of the perfect will of God from this context we are not speaking of the decreed will of God outside of time, which includes all of the actions in time. Although that plan is perfect and will come to pass, it is not that aspect of God's will which Paul refers to in the twelfth chapter of Romans.

We are also not speaking solely of the declared will of God in the Bible, although that, in itself, is perfect.

The perfect will of God spoken of in Romans 12:2 is a more personal matter. It involves God's ideal intent for our lives as we live according to His declared will in the Scriptures. The Scriptures reveal God's expectations, engender faith, and prompt faithful action. The perfect will of God is to personally act out the perfect Word of God.

Romans 12:2 is saying simply that the will of God can be ascertained by the Word of God and put into practice by those who receive it, believe it, and do it. It is something that we have to test, experience, or "prove."

The challenge comes in that none of us are perfect enough to live in the perfect will of God all the time. If the perfect will of God is a life-long standard, we all have missed it. We may not have missed it in major areas of our lives, such as our career calling or in choosing our spouse (although some have failed at those vital points), but we all have fallen short to some degree and in more areas than we may think.

God expresses His perfect intent in the Scriptures. That is the goal. That is the high calling. But then, in grace, He helps us when we miss that touchstone. God helps us to find the greatest degree of blessing possible when we fall short. At the point of failure, the perfect will of God is not lost completely.

In essence, the perfect will of God is a present experience as we take the next step of obedience from wherever we are at the moment.

The life of Moses exemplifies that God's ultimate long-term intent may go unrealized not only because of personal sin but also because of the general relational influence of sin. In other words, Moses missed out on Canaan initially, not because of his own sin, but because of the sin of those whose lives affected his. On the other hand, in the end, he also was not able to enter the Promised Land because of what he himself did. Ultimately, he lost entrance into Canaan by no other fault than his own.

Heaven is where believers will experience God's perfect will all the time. Down here we are always seeking to experience a momentary measure of God's perfect will in a sin-stained environment. This does not have to be a point of depression for us. The encouraging thought here is that we can go forward having a vision of blessing no matter what has happened in the past or no matter what complications and consequences we currently live with due to our sins or the sins of those around us.

Wow! That is a transformational message!

Many Christians live in a state of defeat because they mistakenly think, "It's no use going forward. I've already missed the perfect will of God—there's no hope for me."

We all need to pray like Moses did in Psalm 90. We all need to learn the "Plan B" prayer.

Psalm 90 is a prayer of personal acceptance for an alternate way. It is a prayer anticipating the blessings found in a new direction other than that which we originally expected. As Christians, we need to learn to pray this prayer, not from rote memory, but in principle and spirit. In the end, when we realize that God's sovereign design includes all contingencies, we learn to count "Plan B" as the new "Plan A."

Moses is a great teacher. As a man of God, he was in tune to the movements of God's providence. His life was one of extreme change and variance in circumstantial conditions. Moses' journey took him all over the map. He went up and down, here and there—so close to Canaan, and yet, so far away.

His prayer is a pattern for us. It is especially insightful for the multitude among us who find it challenging to embrace change.

Moses is still leading a multitude. We are the followers. Psalm 90 is the guidebook. This man of God handed down to us a most valuable tool for the Christian pilgrimage.

Let's see what it says.

EXTRA POINTS TO PONDER

Questions

1. What is said of Moses in Numbers 12:3?

He is very meek and above all men.

2. What do Psalm 22:26, 25:9, and 37:11 say God will do for a man like Moses?

He will seek them.

3. To whom is Moses compared in Hebrews 3:1, 2?

Apostle and High Priest, Christ Jesus

4. According to verse 2, what characteristic did they both share?

They were both faithful

5. If even a man like Moses missed out on a measure of God's perfect will, what does that say for us?

6. From Moses' comments in Deuteronomy 32:4, how do you think he responded to God's discipline in his life?

Very well, because he knew what was right from wrong he expected it.

Thought

Moses was a man of great spiritual stature, but even he, at times, fell short of God's will for his life. When we lose the ideal, like Moses, we must respond in meekness looking for the greatest possible degree of blessing in the days ahead. If we grow bitter and resentful or push forward without God, we only make things worse. If we submit in meekness, we can enjoy the presence of God and find surprising blessings ahead.

CHAPTER TWO

THE LORD, OUR DWELLING PLACE

Lord, thou hast been our dwelling place in all generations.—PSALM 90:1

Moses begins his prayer with an acknowledgment of the ever-present essence of God. In our "Plan B" prayer, this is where we must start as well.

In God, "...we live, and move, and have our being" as Paul said and which was so succinctly recorded in Acts 17:28. Only God is infinite and eternal. All life proceeds from Him. He is unique and distinct from the created universe, yet He supports and sustains it through personal attachment and correlative care.

God is everywhere. In Psalm 139, David bears this out when he asks the rhetorical question of God: "Whither shall I go from thy spirit? Or whither shall I flee from thy presence?" David says that he could ascend as far as heaven, and God would be there. He adds that he could make his bed in hell, and God would be there as well (Psalm 139:7–8). The highest heaven contains the throne of God and His special physical presence. Hell beneath is shielded from God's goodness, yet it is sustained by His attending character of wrathful justice. Even in the deepest recesses of the bottomless pit, there is no escaping God. You can't go any higher than Heaven. You can't go any lower than Hell. God's presence extends to both of these extremes.

Depending on our relationship with God, this is either a negative or positive thought. Moses was a man of God. In his mind, the knowledge of God's presence was the primary source of comfort as he lived without a permanent home.

Moses was destined to wander the wilderness leading God's wayward people. He was a man without a country. His was the tent-life. His was the life of a perpetual camping trip—setting up, tearing down, and moving on. I can see why he desperately sought the Lord.

To me, camping is fun at first. Everything looks promising when you get out your gear and begin to form your little fabric fort for the coming days. But inevitably, the experience begins to wear adversely at your spirit—the rain, the bugs, the backache from sleeping on the hard ground.

At its best, camping is short-lived—allowing just enough time to appreciate the great outdoors without becoming angry at it. When you're yelling at the sky and barking at the moon it may be time to look for a Motel 6. When your pack of hotdogs has fallen into the campfire and you're left to scrounge for edible mushrooms or borrow food from any nearby Boy Scout Troop, it is probably time to pack it up and go home.

Can you imagine living forty years in a tent? Can you imagine what it was like for Moses to wander in the wilderness knowing that Canaan was just a few miles away?

Moses had to find his spiritual refuge in something other than his situation. He had to find a settlement and resting place for his soul in a place somewhere...elsewhere. He found his refuge in God.

Moses was well aware of Israel's history. He knew the heritage of the patriarchs of God's people starting with Abraham. All of them were wanderers. They all had to find their refuge in God. Moses looked back before he looked forward. He pulled from the experience of those before him and related it to his own.

Through meditation on God's revelation, he was able to discern that all of this life is transient. As created beings, our life is characterized by constant change. Every day we experience the process of succession. We are living while we are dying. We are adding and losing at the same time. We live in a body—a tent for our soul that is wearing out. It is not equipped to long withstand the elements. Every generation, no matter how stable and seemingly secure, is moving towards replacement. Even the oldest men recorded in the Bible lived and died taking up a brief notation in the eternal record. Only

God can provide security during this short stay on earth. He is a refuge. He is a home.

You see, the phrase "dwelling place" used by Moses does not only denote physical existence but also spiritual security.

Although it is true that we live in the presence of God, we cannot find refuge in that experience unless we are relationally close to God. We may be physically close to God's sustaining presence but not relationally close. We can be close to God physically, but yet, so far away spiritually.

God only becomes a refuge when we are in close communion with Him. When fellowship is unobstructed and clear, the result is a deep, settled peace in our spirit. God is close to us in our hearts, and our hearts find a true dwelling place and home in Him.

In his epistle, James talks about relational closeness to God. He provokes believers by saying, "Draw nigh to God, and he will draw nigh to you" (James 4:8). In this context, God's people were worldly—finding their satisfaction in the things of the world instead of in their relationship with God. Because of this, their prayers were not being answered by God. God was resisting them (James 4:1–6).

James tells them that they must repent and remove the sins that were hindering close fellowship with God. He said, "Cleanse your hands, ye sinners; and purify your hearts, ye double minded" (verse 8 again). These wayward Christians were not only involved in sin, but also they were seeking a refuge in the world. This caused them to be double-minded.

They were trying to tune in to two channels at once. In the process, they could not hear the voice of God inside them.

This is simple to illustrate: If I am riding down the interstate listening to a good sermon on a good Christian radio station, the sound only stays strong as I travel within range of the broadcast signal. If I start to hear another channel come in, I am too far from the original station tower. Soon, the sermon will become muddled by the sound of a country twang, heavy metal bang, or non-stop hip hop beat. When a bellowing pop diva starts to sing a rousing retro tune, there is no way I can concentrate; there is no way to hear the preacher on the dial. If I want to listen to the sermon clearly, I only have one choice: I must turn around and drive back towards the preferred station.

Here's the correlation: In sin, many Christians turn to the world for satisfaction. They fill their spiritual ears with the messages of the world—audible, visible, and philosophical. In so doing, they spiritually move away from God. Only when they draw close to God can the peace of God, which surpasses understanding, keep and guard their hearts and minds (Philippians 4:7).

God is everywhere, but we must maintain relational closeness to Him to experience His peace on the alternative paths we take. When life does not turn out as we expect, when our earthly security is in jeopardy, we must learn to rediscover our secure base in God Himself.

David knew what it meant to be close to God. No wonder he spoke of God as his "hiding place," "refuge," and "habitation" (Psalms 32:7, 62:7, and 71:3).

Like Moses, David knew what it was like to live for a time with conditions far more austere than he expected. He took a detour of sorts.

David was anointed as the new king of Israel but was delayed in experiencing the fruition of his calling. He had to run for his life as the present king sought to kill him. He lived in caves. He looked for refuge in hard desert places. He even went into foreign territory seeking to find respite. In his life on the run, he was able to find a refuge in his relationship with God. He walked with God, talked with God, sang to God, and poured out his complaint to God. To him, God was a "very present help in trouble" (Psalm 46:1).

God is always there for His people.

For Moses and the children of Israel, God was not waiting in Canaan. God was with them and would remain with them in the wilderness. Moses began his prayer with this realization as a starting point.

Without this realization, all prayer degenerates into a pathetic, dutiful expression. We have to believe that God is with us. To pray in sincerity, we have to believe that God is as close as the air we breathe.

At the inception of this kind of faith, we find a foundation to hold up the structure of all our praise and heartfelt requests. True prayer cannot begin until, by faith, we become aware of the presence of God. When we realize that He is our dwelling place, what's ahead does not look so daunting. Every step simply provides an opportunity to delve into another dimension of His presence. His grace is made available for the present need, and we are able to take on any challenge and walk forward by faith. His presence guarantees our future security.

In this first verse, we find an amazing initial perception that stirs our interest in what is to come.

The Lord is our dwelling place. What a profound reflection!

If, by the inspiration of the Holy Spirit, Moses could lead us that far in a few short words, what great nuggets of truth will be revealed to us as we consider the words to follow?

EXTRA POINTS TO PONDER

Questions

1. What do Colossians 1:17 and Hebrews 1:3 say about how the universe is supported?

2. What does Jeremiah 23:24 say about God?

3. With these facts in view, is Hebrews 13:5 a realistic promise?

4. According to Matthew 18:20, where can we experience God's special presence?

5. If we are not sensing God's presence in our lives, what may be the case (2 Chronicles 15:2)?

6. If we do seek God, what will He be to us in times of trouble and turmoil (Psalm 62:8)?

Thought

God is with us. That is a fact that we must not forget when we take a detour from the path of ideal blessing. We may be on a different road, but that does not mean God has left us to fend for ourselves. He is still there. And when we reckon this to be so, we will come to know a closer communion with God than we would have ever thought possible in the place where we find ourselves.

CHAPTER THREE

FROM EVERLASTING TO EVERLASTING

Before the mountains were brought forth, or ever thou hadst formed the earth and the world, even from everlasting to everlasting, thou art God.—PSALM 90:2

The first thing that stands out from this verse is the clear statement concerning God's creative work in the universe. God exists prior to (from man's perspective) the creation of the earth and the greater world being the infinite First Cause of it all.

We expect this to be true because no suggested alternative will do. The universe did not create itself, and everything could not have been preceded by nothing. Someone or something must be infinite. And since we find personality, intellect, beauty, and morality in the created world, the First Cause must possess all of these attributes to design them in reflective form.

There must be a God!

And only the God revealed in the Bible and in the person of Jesus Christ has the character and credentials to be so. He is the Divine Creator who exists and operates outside the bounds of time and space. He "inhabits eternity" (Isaiah 57:15).

It hurts our heads to even consider this truth. How do we wrap our minds around eternity? We can't fully, but we must try. At least, we can get closer than we are in our normal, indifferent state. Our minds may spin a bit, but we must contemplate God's eternal nature to some extent in our little, finite minds if we are going to get a true perspective of our temporal condition.

This is especially needful when we are forced to take an exit on the road to the ideal.

At the outset of this prayer, Moses reminds himself of the transcendent truth of God's eternal, immutable nature. He had a special awareness of this fact. After all, Moses was the one to whom God first revealed Himself as the Great "I AM" (Exodus 3:14). This is an amazing present-tense designation. This title speaks of self-sufficiency and independent existence. It also speaks of that which transcends time.

Time is a succession of moments. The succession of time denotes either development or decay. God has no such succession. He neither develops nor decays. God lives in a perfect, unconditioned, and immutable state.

When Genesis 1:1 says, "In the beginning God…," it does not mean only that God existed before the beginning but that God exists beyond the beginning. His existence stretches to the far reaches of both the past and the future all at once. He is ever-present.

The full knowledge of this is too wonderful for us mere mortals, but whatever degree we can ascend closer to it will go a long way in determining how we think about our short lives.

When God revealed this name "I AM" to Moses, it was at the time when Moses was being called to lead the nation of Israel out of Egypt. Moses felt completely insufficient for the task. Exodus 3:11 records that Moses said to God, "Who am I, that I should go unto Pharaoh, and that I should bring forth the children of Israel out of Egypt?"

God did not answer him by saying, "You're number one!" "You are something!" or "You can do it!" Instead God answered, "...Certainly, I will be with you..." (Exodus 3:12). And then He said, "Tell them that I AM has sent you" (Exodus 3:14, my paraphrase).

Moses was a humble man. Also, he was experiencing a stubborn case of self-doubt. God knew that what Moses needed to go forward was not a better estimation of himself; what he needed was a better estimation of God. In expressing His eternal nature, God gave Moses more than enough means for confidence in his calling.

Our world is telling us that our confidence must be in ourselves. We need a better "self-image," they say.

Certainly we should not deplore ourselves. The Bible assumes the fact that self-love is natural. God tells us to love our neighbors as ourselves (Matthew 19:19, 22:39; Mark 12:31; and Luke 10:29). But this natural affection for ourselves can easily devolve into conceit and a presumptuous sense of self-sufficiency. That is the form of self-love denounced in 2 Timothy 3:2 when Paul describes the mindset of the last days and says that "men shall be lovers of their own selves."

To have a proper estimation of ourselves and strike the balance, we must have a proper estimation of our eternal Creator. God does not want us to deplore ourselves but depend on Him.

First and foremost, we need a better "God-image"!

Our being is rooted in Him. Our confidence is in His calling for our lives. And since that calling supersedes time, we can be assured that we are invincible until we finish what He has designed for us to do.

These thoughts, derived from Psalm 90 and other passages, were a source of blessing for me during some very dark days.

After my cancer diagnosis in 2009, I endured almost a year of treatments including radiation, five rounds of chemotherapy, and a stem cell transplant. The discomfort seemed endless at the time. Looking forward, I could see only more pain. My doctors told me that in time I could expect a good result, but it's hard to see the future when the present is so all-consuming. After the stem cell transplant, I was told that I could expect to be out of commission for six months.

"Six months?!" I said to myself. Six months seemed like an eternity especially since I could not perform my duties as a pastor and would be quarantined at home most of the time.

Amazingly, God shored up my spirit through His Word. I began to value every moment. I found tasks which I could tackle within my limits. I wrote messages and included them in an online blog. I exercised as much as possible. I spent quality time with my wife and kids for extended periods not always available in the past.

In an amazing turn of events about four weeks after my stem cell transplant, I had the worst day ever. My hair was gone. My stomach was in turmoil. My taste buds were not working, and I was experiencing weird cerebral sensations as if I were losing control of my mind. I wanted to die. Somehow, I made it through the day. Waking up the next morning, I felt completely normal. I felt fine. Actually, I felt better than fine—I felt one hundred percent again. It was amazing! I still had no hair and little taste, but I felt invigorated and strong. I felt like a new man. I felt the same way the next day, and the next, and the next. I told my wife, "There is no way I can stay home from church now when I am feeling this good."

After convincing the doctors that I would be careful, I received the go-ahead to return to work. Our church was in shock when I walked into the congregation after six weeks instead of six months.

It's been over four years since then, and I have never felt better. The year of treatment now seems like a distant dream. I look at pictures of myself back then, and it seems unreal. What at first appeared as if it would last forever, turned out to be a few frames on the movie screen of my life. There may be more dark days ahead, but I think I am more prepared in perspective to endure them. In contemplating God's eternity, I have become more sensitive to the temporal nature of this life and less impacted by its trials.

It is no wonder that at this time of transition and during his trial, Moses reminded himself of the eternal nature of God. How could he otherwise see value in going back into the wilderness without recognizing the perfection of God's eternal purpose based on the immutability of His timeless being?

He couldn't look around for encouragement. He had to look up.

For Moses, the truth of God's eternality also provided a backdrop to compare and contrast the limitations and frailty of human life.

What's ahead in the psalm is not a pretty picture, for sure. The middle section of the psalm expresses a realistic view of the frustrations of living in a world characterized by the curse of sin. Those who falsely glamorize this life are destined to be disappointed by unrealized expectations. Those who see earthly life for what it is are drawn to hope in God. They do not drown in despair. Get ready for a somber estimation of our earthly existence. Verses 3–11 break through the "Hollywood hype" of endless days of fun in the sun and tell us the sober truth about the hardships we face here on earth. But at least verses 1–2 provide a positive point of reference to elevate the evaluation of our otherwise hopeless experience. Moses comes back to that in the end.

Stay tuned.

EXTRA POINTS TO PONDER

Questions

1. What does Isaiah 57:15 say about God's nature?

2. What does Genesis 1:1 assume about God's existence?

3. Can the same thing be said about Jesus Christ (John 1:1; Colossians 1:16, 17)?

4. Based on this, how could Jesus take all of our eternal sin debt on Himself on the cross?

5. What does contemplating God's eternal nature do for us (See Isaiah 26:3–4)?

Thought

Thoughts of God's eternal nature are hard thoughts. They do not come naturally. Only through an intensive gaze into God's Word can we arrive at some degree of recognition of and appreciation for the majestic truth. But when we do, our temporal trials do not seem so great. The perishing vanities of this world do not seem so tempting. We discard our own selfish desires when lost in the wonder of God's immense and all-encompassing will. Like Moses, we elevate our thinking in this way at the time when our lives take a turn in an unplanned and unwanted direction.

CHAPTER FOUR

TURN AND RETURN

Thou turnest man to destruction; and sayest, Return, ye children of men.—PSALM 90:3

This is a curious verse, isn't it?

Moses says that God turns man to destruction and tells the children of men to return.

What does it mean? It seems as if God forces us to turn from what might otherwise be a source of life so that we return to the dust from which we came.

I think Moses is speaking of the stark reality that God has determined to allow the curse of sin to follow its course and take its toll on the lives of all who walk the earth. In other words, we all must succumb to death. And although death may seem like a random bandit stealing lives arbitrarily, it is not.

This verse says that God is doing more than allowing death to take its toll. He is actively involved in the transaction. God is not passively watching the consequence. He is the one saying, "Turn and return!"

In the immediate context, God was telling Moses and a generation of the nation of Israel to turn from Canaan to return to the wilderness where they would eventually expire. In a general sense, God has a hand in the death of all people.

Some see this as an indictment against God. They see God as a malicious murderer since He is actively involved in the death of men and the children of men.

I submit that the real indictment would be if He were passive not active. If God has a "hands-off" approach to life and death, it would mean that He either chooses to watch us suffer indiscriminate pain or that He chooses not to watch us at all. If God is passive, then there are no redeeming qualities to suffering and death, and He is either indolent, infirmed, or uninterested. The Bible does not let us believe that.

What the Bible does say is that God is sovereign over all, and His kingdom rules over all things (Psalm 103:19). If God is sovereign over everything, certainly He must be in control over life and death. In Deuteronomy 32:39, He said to the nation of Israel, "…I kill, and I make alive…." He repeats the same in 1 Samuel 2:6 just in case we did not get it the first time. Job understood this reality when at the loss of his family he said, "…the Lord gave, and the Lord hath taken away…" (Job 1:21). Paul understood it when he explained that God has given all men "life and breath" and has "determined" the "bounds of their habitation" (Acts 17:25–26). If not even a sparrow can fall to the ground and die unless it is according to the Father's wisdom and will (Matthew 10:29), how much more is God involved in the times and passing seasons of each human person?

Before we misinterpret this sovereignty as mere arbitrary determinism, we must understand that God's will outside of time involves the movements of time and includes responding to man in time. I do not presume to know how this works, but God tells me in His Word that it does. I don't have to reconcile this; for faith, I just have to reckon it to be so. If it were not so, God would be accusable of evil.

God did not bring the curse of death by mere determinism. He warned Adam in the Garden not to disobey which would result in the curse of death. God expressed His desire that Adam do what was right. Why would God do that unless there was some relational and responsive quality to His will? There must be, otherwise Adam would not be responsible. But he was, and is.

God said to Adam after he sinned, "...cursed is the ground for thy sake..." and "In the sweat of thy face shalt thou eat bread, till thou return unto the ground..." (Genesis 3:17 and 19). Adam was responsible because he was able to respond to God, and God was righteous in that He was able to respond to Adam in a way not inconsistent with His sovereign purpose and power.

God does not turn us back to dust for no good reason. Whenever death happens, God is working with infallible intuition and pure wisdom to bring about what is right and best in relation to man's existence, individually and corporately. We might not know at the moment what that right reason is, but He does. We must believe that. If we do, then the reality of death will not turn us away from God but will, on the contrary, attract us to Him and His saving grace.

We could believe with the naturalist and materialist that death is insignificant and ultimately meaningless. But to go there, we must believe that life is meaningless as well.

If we are simply material beings and our members contain no spiritual animation but only exist physically and wear out like the components of a computer, what is there to prompt our instinctive preference for worth in this world? Everything means nothing. We are just biological byproducts of the cosmos destined for the junk heap of universal decomposition. Even if there is some form of reproductive recycling that occurs after we die, without true spiritual and conscious life, what does it matter?

Surely, we cannot believe that. It would be without good sense, and to do so is to accept a notion of utter hopelessness.

The Bible says that man was made in God's image—in God's likeness. We are not God but are a reflection of the divine personality being three-part beings with moral awareness (1 Thessalonians 5:23, Genesis 3:22). When God made the plants and the animals, He simply spoke them into existence. But when He made man, He stopped, slowed down, formed him from the dust of the ground, and breathed into his nostrils. At that point, man became a living soul (Genesis 1:27).

The truth is that the death of any man is tragic because his life contains a degree of divine likeness and spiritual essence and is therefore significant and sacred.

The tragedy of death is only diminished by the well-founded affirmation that the God who gave life on earth certainly has the right to determine the limits of that existence. When life ceases for any individual it is according to His perfect design and a consummately, righteous end. If we can praise the Lord for life, we can praise the Lord in death.

Job did.

Job praised the Lord when faced with the death of his children. Not only did he say, "...the Lord gave, and the Lord hath taken away," but he added, "blessed be the name of the Lord" (Job 1:21).

God is turning us to the destruction of death, but that is not to say that we will cease to exist. Physical death is the separation of the soul from the body. The soul continues in a state of conscious existence after physical death. Solomon spoke of this fact in Ecclesiastes 12:7 when he said of death, "Then shall the dust return to the earth as it was: and the spirit shall return unto God who gave it."

Not only is that true, but according to the Bible, the soul disembodied from its earthly house will be contained in some temporary body until the resurrection of the earthly to its reconstructed eternal state (Luke 16:19–31, Daniel 12:2, 1 Corinthians 15:35–49). We who know Christ as our Saviour have a glorified body that we can look forward to—one that is incorruptible. I take that to mean that there will be no more stomach aches, tooth aches, and back aches—no hair loss, memory loss, and hearing loss.... (Need I go on?) We wait for the day when we put on our glorified bodies. Until then, the soul is always contained in some temporary corporeal form (Matthew 17:1–4).

For the born-again believer in Jesus Christ, God assures us that the moment we die we will be with Him in Heaven.

To the believing thief on the cross next to Him, Jesus said, "*Today* shalt thou be with me in paradise" (Luke 23:43).

As Stephen was about to die, he said, "Behold, I see the heavens opened, and the Son of man standing on the right hand of God." And just before he breathed his last breath he cried, "Lord Jesus, receive my spirit" (Acts 7:56, 59). Paul expressed his longing to be "with Christ" at death (Philippians 1:23) and affirmed his assurance that "...to be absent from the body" means to "...be present with the Lord" (2 Corinthians 5:8).

Having this confidence we can say, "O death, where is thy sting? O grave, where is thy victory?" (1 Corinthians 15:55).

Among other things, praying the "Plan B" prayer means that we must come to terms with the inevitable nature of death, and that God is in control of it all. We cannot refuse to acknowledge that death exists. We cannot ignore it. We cannot dissuade ourselves from facing it.

Death is the ultimate interruption of the ideal. It is the final intrusion on our plans and to our endeavors. When we face its reality head on and see God's sovereignty in it, we are freed from fear to really live with whatever challenge is before us at the moment. If God wants us to die, we will die. If God wants us to live, we will live. As believers, let's get over the fear and go forward.

Moses needed this perspective to face what he had to face, and so do we.

It will take a few more verses to fully work it out so we cannot stop now. The next verse builds on what we just learned.

EXTRA POINTS TO PONDER

Questions

1. What stark reality does Solomon discuss in Ecclesiastes 9:9? Is he discussing this from an earthly or an eternal perspective?

2. What should the inevitable nature of this reality cause us to do (Ecclesiastes 9:10)?

3. Looking at Ecclesiastes 9:11–12 from an earthly perspective, are we ever going to be able to reconcile all of this life's apparent inequities and contrasting outcomes?

4. According to Ecclesiastes 9:12, what do we not know in this life?

5. Who knows what we do not know (Job 14:1–5)?

Thought

It never helps us to fret about the day of our death. Nor does it pay to pine away dreaming of an elusive utopia on earth. It is more profitable to focus our time and attention on the day we have and the task at hand. Knowing that God is with us now and that He knows our future appointment in the air is sufficient for us to have confidence to give our whole hearts to whatever God's will is for the moment.

CHAPTER FIVE

FROM HERE TO ETERNITY

For a thousand years in thy sight are but as yesterday when it is past, and as a watch in the night.—PSALM 90:4

Punctuality is a companion characteristic to the traits of discipline, order, and virtue. Some among us berate punctuality. To some, being late is fashionable—that is, until one of the typically tardy travelers is waiting on someone else. Then watch out for the fit of frustration! Everyone hates to wait. We all have experienced the agony of waiting on others. We all know how torturously time can creep by when we are in a holding pattern of imposed delay.

When our church started in September 1999, we had twenty-five people in the inaugural service. Most of those arrived five to ten minutes late—some even longer.

I will never forget standing at the door waiting for the first potential congregants to arrive. Stacie and I had left our comfortable ministry in North Carolina to plant a church in Connecticut. For six months, we had been planning and preparing for this day. We advertised by mail and newspaper and by organizing a forty-thousand-piece flyer distribution effort door to door in our community. This opening day was the culmination of many hours of hard work. Five minutes before the service was to start, there were only five people present—all who were related to me. I thought to myself, "Great! This thing is going to flop!" Also I was thinking that I would have to write to tell our financial supporters that nothing happened. Maybe I could baptize my mother-in-law just for something to do. But then one car drove up and then another.

Slowly but surely, a small group gathered. Why were they so late? Did they not know what they were doing to me? Obviously, they weren't as anxious and excited as I. They weren't operating on my schedule. In the end, I just was glad they came.

It's been thirteen years since that day. People are still late to church. I wish I could say that I am more accustomed to it, but I am not. It drives me batty!

One time, I called for an electrical repair appointment at the church building. The repairman said that he would be there between 9:00 and 11:00 AM. Since I had to be there to open the doors for him, I arrived promptly at nine. Finally, he arrived at 12:30 PM and only after three increasingly incensed messages by phone to motivate him. I should have known. Most repairmen live with a different sense of schedule than the rest of us. Waiting on repairmen ranks right up there with going to a doctor's appointment or waiting in line at the Department of Motor Vehicles.

According to Moses in Psalm 90:4, God also operates with a different understanding of time. A day to God is as a thousand years, and a thousand years is as a day, as 2 Peter 3:8 confirms. And if, as Moses states, a thousand years to God is like yesterday when it is passed, why would He be in a hurry with anything He does?

God is never in a rush. He always takes His time.

This does not mean God is not punctual. It simply means He is on a different schedule than ours. It may seem as if He is lingering. It may seem that He is not on time, but He is. He just does not conform to our schedule of expectations.

Does this mean God is oblivious to time as we see it? Does it mean He does not care about the constrictions of our short lives? Does He somehow get pleasure from the fact that we have to wait in anguish for His purposes to be made known?

Moses put in many years of service with one goal in mind—making it to Canaan, only to be turned back twice. Moses had to return to the wilderness with a murmuring people. He asked the question, "How long is this going to last?" (verse 13), and certainly he added, "What is the purpose of this long trial?"

Was God manipulating the mind of Moses? Does God not understand how important some attainments are for us mortals who live in a place where every moment counts and where death casts such a dark shadow over every day?

Certainly He does, but it is going to take a trip from here to eternity and back in order to ascertain how.

First of all, to come to some understanding of God's perspective of time, it is important to realize that in creation God constrained Himself to the limits of time. He did not have to create the world in six literal, twenty-four-hour days, but He did. There is nothing in the creation passages of Genesis 1–3 to indicate otherwise.

Some people try so hard to impose evolution on the creation account. To do so, they must do some exegetical gymnastics. They combine the truth with secular thought and tie it in knots. And if what they conclude about the story is true (which it's not), God was trying to trick the general reader with the seemingly clear statements contained therein.

God did not employ evolution to create the world, and He did not need to. He did not need to employ any significant time. He could have created it all at once. If He so desires, God can do an eternity of work in one second of time. (Is that not what Jesus did on the cross? If He took the full weight of the everlasting punishment of sin and Hell on Himself for the whole world, He had to do so by pulling eternity into the framework of time and space. Amazing!) The reason stated as to why God worked in six days was to set a pattern of work and rest for man (Exodus 20:11).

This is instructive because it shows that God can relate to working in the realm of time. He knows what it means to work the process of His purpose in a succession of order and development. He knows Himself what it means to wait.

God has to wait on us, does He not? First Peter 3:20 tells us that God, in longsuffering, waited in the days of Noah while the ark was being prepared. What was He waiting for? He was waiting for Noah to finish the boat. Also, He was enduring with much patience the rebellion of mankind while in mercy offering those alive to hear a 120-year message of deliverance. And ultimately, He was waiting for His perfect purpose to be realized on the earth. How could God be longsuffering without having some duration with which to deal?

Isaiah 30:18 is a curious verse on this point. It says, "And therefore will the Lord wait, that he may be gracious unto you, and therefore will he be exalted, that he may have mercy upon you: for the Lord is a God of judgment: blessed are all they that wait for him." What does this mean?

Is it some anthropomorphic expression to say that God waits? Is it just an accommodation of language so that we can relate to God?

In its context, Isaiah 30:18 means that God was graciously patient with the nation of Israel in allowing them time to return to Him before His full judgment would begin in destroying their homeland and scattering them throughout the world. The amazing truth is that the revelation of Him waiting on His people provides the impulse and motivation for His people to wait on Him.

This all says that God is doing a patient work in the world that involves responding in time to the movements of man.

Somehow responding to man does not conflict with His sovereign plan formed and framed outside of time. We wait on Him, understanding that He is waiting for the perfect, particular fulfillment of all His purpose. This revelation of God cannot be an anthropomorphic accommodation to our mind, as if God is metaphorically ascribing to Himself human characteristics. God has chosen to operate in time. Because of such, He has to wait.

Certainly, Jesus knew what it meant to wait.

Jesus is God in the flesh (John 1:14). He waited on people. He waited for provision—forty days for food at one point in His life (Matthew 4:1–11). (Amazing! I can hardly wait after lunch for my midafternoon snack. When I do fast, it is through a meal or two—a day or two on rare occasions.) Jesus endured the cross and the painful trials of the day leading up to it. And this was all fulfilled because God the Father waited for thousands of years for the fullness of time to send His Son to be the Saviour of the world. No wonder the fruit of the Spirit is patience (Galatians 5:22), because God knows how to wait.

So what is the difference between God and us in relation to time? The difference is that God is not preoccupied with passing moments because He sees the fullness of time and the eternal purpose of all things in one panoramic view. He is able to traverse from here to eternity with perfect precision. Somehow, He is able to work in time without strained limitation, anxiety, and doubt. In this way, He is so unlike us. That is why we need His perspective that He offers us by His revelation. If a thousand years is like a passing day to

Him, certainly He sees the big picture. He can help us get a glimpse of that portrait as well. When we do, we won't have to be absorbed with the past as if there is something we can do about it or as if the past is determinative of the future.

With this perspective, we also will look at the present differently. We won't have to see the entire fulfillment of God's promises completely packaged for the here and now. We won't expect every prayer to be answered immediately. (This expectation would bring perpetual discontentment.) And we will not have to look to the future with fear.

All we need to know is that God holds all time in His hands. Uncertainty is only in our minds, not His. We can live with peace, hope, and joy knowing that God will help us deal with the challenge at hand and that eternity fills the present moment with purpose.

Now we know why Moses spoke from here to eternity in his poetic prayer. He needed a look at the big picture so as to face another day. As he looked out into the wilderness thinking what might be waiting there for years to come, he had to look up so as not to be distracted from the peace that comes in knowing that God's purpose was much larger than his life and was being perfectly executed in time.

EXTRA POINTS TO PONDER

Questions

1. What part of God's plan was made secret since the world began (Romans 16:25, Ephesians 1:9, 10; 3:1–6)?

2. Who made the command that this "mystery" should be manifest in time (Romans 16:25): "the __________ God"?

3. When did this mysterious manifestation happen according to Ephesians 1:10: "…in the ________________ of times"?

4. Do you think everything in God's plan happens in this manner (Galatians 4:4)?

5. With David, what will we say in light of this knowledge (Psalm 31:15)?

Thought

God's eternal plan was conceived outside the bounds of time on earth; therefore, God's plan is proceeding right on schedule in that time only makes manifest what has been ordained to be so in eternity. This plan includes His responses in time to our actions and ways. With this in mind, we can go forward with perfect confidence in God's timing.

CHAPTER SIX

THE DANGEROUS DISPLEASURE OF GOD

Thou carriest them away as with a flood; they are as a sleep: in the morning they are like grass which groweth up. In the morning it flourisheth, and groweth up; in the evening it is cut down, and withereth. For we are consumed by thine anger, and by thy wrath are we troubled. Thou hast set our iniquities before thee, our secret sins in the light of thy countenance. For all our days are passed away in thy wrath...—PSALM 90:5–9

Some who presume to speak for God tell us that, as Christians, we do not have to fear the Lord. They say that if we know God's love completely, it is unnecessary that we fear Him.

"Doesn't 1 John 4:18 state 'perfect love casteth out fear?'" they argue.

Taken out of its context, it may be construed to mean that, but in light of the surrounding passage, 1 John 4:18 is clear. In context, this verse means that if a person exhibits the characteristic signs of a true believer, he does not need to fear the final judgment of God. He has "...boldness in the day of judgment..." (verse 17). One of the characteristics of a true believer is a love for God and a love for the brethren (verses 19–20). In other words, with the assurance of salvation exemplified by Christian love, we have no reason to fear the torment of eternal punishment for sin in Hell.

First John 4:18 in no way teaches that a Christian should never dread the awful displeasure and discipline of God. On the contrary, 2 Corinthians 7:1 tells believers to perfect "...holiness in the fear of God." Ephesians 5:21 instructs, "Submit...one to another in the fear of God." In Philippians 2:12 the apostle Paul prompts Christians by saying, "work out your own salvation with fear and trembling." The writer of Hebrews adds that grace actually causes a healthy fear of the Lord when he writes, "...have grace, whereby we may serve God acceptably with reverence and godly fear" (Hebrews 12:28). The apostle Peter concludes that we should "...pass the time of your sojourning here in fear" (1 Peter 1:17).

The same false teachers previously mentioned are the ones promoting the idea that fellow ministers should only speak about the positive love of God.

"It's all about His love," they say. "All we need is love—love! love! love!"

These pretentious preachers rarely, if ever, speak of Hell. They seldom speak of a judgment to come. They ignore the hard truths of the Bible and talk, predominately, of God's unconditional love and acceptance, which they say means that He has a wonderful purpose of prosperity for everyone.

"We are living in the age of grace," they say, as if grace is some soupy softness that overlooks every evil way and focuses only on the good.

Why is it then that Jesus spoke more about Hell than He did Heaven? (Count up the times, and see if I'm right.) Why is it that Jesus used His ability to destroy our bodies in Hell as a means to motivate both believers and unbelievers? In Luke 12:4–5 He said to a multitude (including His disciples), "...Be not afraid of them that kill the body, and after that have no more that they can do. But I will forewarn you whom ye shall fear: Fear him, which after he hath killed hath power to cast into hell; yea, I say unto you, Fear him."

God loves the world enough that He provided a way of salvation from the eternal penalty of sin through the sacrifice of Jesus on the cross. He does love with a special affection those who come to Him in faith and are adopted into His family. But we must not forget His wrath poured out in punishment of sin. And we must not confuse His unconditional acceptance in Christ with His conditional favor and, conversely, the broken fellowship with God that we can experience due to our bad behavior.

Hebrews 10:30 cites Deuteronomy 32:36 when it says, "The Lord shall judge his people." The next verse in Hebrews adds, "It is a fearful thing to fall into the hands of the living God." The judgment of God upon His people is an Old and New Testament concept then.

First Corinthians 11:30 says that due to regarded sin and the taking of the Lord's Supper in a dishonoring manner, "many" Christians "are weak and sickly…and many sleep." We are then told to "judge ourselves" so that "we should not be judged" by God (vs. 31). The apostle John says to Christians in his first epistle that "there is a sin unto death" (1 John 5:16). God is trying to tell us that, even as His children, we should always remember that His displeasure is dangerous.

I know. This is not fun to hear. It's not fun to say either. But it is true, nonetheless.

Not only should Christians love the Lord, but also they should fear Him by having a healthy apprehension of His correction. Fear and love are not mutually exclusive. Moses knew this. He told the nation of Israel in Deuteronomy 10:12, "…what doth the Lord thy God require of thee, but to fear the Lord…and to love him…." Psalm 112:1 says that a righteous man will fear the Lord and delight greatly in His commandments. Fear and love—fear and delight; they go together. In the New Testament era, we can expect that by grace and through justification we can live in this conjoined condition.

I think of this dual sense of love and fear as being similar to my sentiments towards my earthly father.

I loved my dad, but I feared his anger and discipline. My dad was a pastor for many years. He believed the biblical admonitions concerning how to correct children. He believed in spanking. (Oh no! I can hear the loud siren of the "politically correct police"!) My dad was old school in this matter, literally. In fact, when he was a public school teacher before entering the pastoral ministry, he used a paddle in the classroom to correct his students for direct disobedience and defiance. I know that this is taboo today, but it works if done in love and restraint (and on the cushy backside target where there is little risk of permanent damage). In his school, he was encouraged to do so by the principal. The school custodian even crafted a paddle for Dad that would be effective.

My dad's spanking apparatus was made of plywood. It had a wide contact surface with an aerodynamic design having holes drilled through the face so that it could pass through the air quickly. It was a masterpiece of engineering. On the front, my dad wrote the words, "Board of Education." How appropriate, because this paddling device was a great teacher. (Believe me, I know first hand—you know, by feeling its corrective warmth down there where the sun don't shine.)

You see, not only did Dad use it at school, but he also used it at home. When my brother, sister, or I were involved in rebellious activity, Dad would call us to his bedroom, tell us to bend over, and apply the "board of education to the seat of learning." I can feel it now just thinking about it. This he did early and often, as needed. It did not take long for me to realize that insubordination did not pay.

As we grew, if we happened to forget that lesson, we would face the pain of a loss of privilege or restricted activity. I remember spending many an hour confined to my bedroom as the teen world around me was having a good time somewhere else. This punishment was hard, and it hurt. In time, I grew to realize that to really love my father was to hate that which would displease him. It was my fear for his displeasure that fostered that kind of love and kept me in the path of favor. The same is true in my relationship with God.

If God's people do not have to fear Him, it is obvious from Psalm 90 that Moses did not get the memo. Moses was witnessing the dangerous displeasure of God every day as he watched his own people die in the desert due to their unbelief.

In verses five and six of the psalm, he compares the judgment of God, in general and on his people in particular, to three things: a flood, a night of sleep, and to grass that grows up and is quickly cut down and withered.

The reference to a flood probably relates to the fact that many were being swiftly taken in death. Plagues infected the Israelites in the desert. A whole generation passed in less than forty years—a wholesale wiping away of about a million or more people. God's wrath was being poured out like a torrent of water carrying away a multitude in its path.

A "sleep" relates to the fact that the lives of those taken seemed as short as a passing night in bed. When one is really tired, it is as if just as they close their eyes, their eyes are opening again. This is how many were dying under God's hand. In a snap of the fingers, in a flash, lives were being cut short like a sleep.

The analogy to grass is so fitting following these thoughts. In one short desert day, grass grows up from an unexpected rain and is soon baked by the sun and passes by evening. All of this death and dying caused Moses to say in verse 9, "…all our days are passed away in thy wrath."

This act of extreme discipline seems harsh. Why would God do this?

Verse eight of the psalm gives the answer. It accounts for the fact that God not only saw the open acts of repeated rebellion and unbelief done by His people, but He also knew of the hidden hearts of undutiful doubt and wickedness. All sin is revealed in the light of His countenance. This Moses understood.

Moses understood the compounding consequence of collective objection to God. God heard the people of Israel complain. He heard their constant rebellious thoughts as they said within themselves, "Why did Moses bring us out here? This Promised Land place is not worth the trouble!" So God in His righteous anger confirmed a condition that existed in their hearts and gave them of the fruit of their minds and lips by banishing them from Canaan. The psalmist wrote in Psalm 95:10–11 that God, in response to the rebellion of His people, said to Himself, "Forty years long was I grieved with this generation, and said, It is a people that do err in their heart, and they have not known my ways: Unto whom I sware in my wrath that they should not enter into my rest." Becoming the focus of His indignation, the Jews of which He was speaking walked the wilderness waiting to die.

Moses lived longer than most of those who died in the desert, and yet, he saw his day coming also when he penned these words. In this psalm, the impression is that he too looked to the skies and spotted a gathering cloud developing over him. Death was tracking his every move. Death was breathing its warm breath down his neck. The Grim Reaper was walking a short step behind him. Moses knew full well why. He had disobeyed God publicly, and God was seriously displeased. At this point, it was useless to appeal (although he did try, Deuteronomy 3:23–25). He had to face what was ahead for both him and the people that he was leading.

When we find ourselves on the alternative path, it may be that we have to face the discipline of God and even the looming specter of death in kind. Death must come, in general, due to the displeasure of God against all sin. Sometimes, in particular, it comes because, like the Israelites and Moses, we either have presumptuously flouted the goodness of God or directly disobeyed at points in our lives. We may not know the exact reason why it comes when it comes, but one thing is for sure—death is coming. In the meantime, we must sow what we reap in this life.

How do we go forward when we know that in time serious consequence and even death is waiting for us? We can proceed from where we are only if we accept the inevitable effect of our sin. Ignoring our just due is foolish. Resisting is futile. Embracing the challenge and change that consequence brings is the only way to progress. We must pray "I accept this." This is the basic beginning of the "Plan B" prayer.

Before Moses could look positively upon his situation, he had to be realistic about what that situation entailed. He was in a place of providential reprisal. He had to see it for what it was—a hard time dealt out by God.

At the same time, in order to be diligent with his desire for blessing, Moses had to become acutely aware of the brevity of life. This was not difficult as the passing funeral processionals grew more frequent in the wilderness. A short but serious concentrated pause to think about these hard truths was all that he needed to venture forward with faith and diligence.

The positive prayer is coming later in the psalm, but until then—a few more words of woe.

EXTRA POINTS TO PONDER

Questions

1. According to Hebrews 12:6, why does the Lord discipline His children?

2. Can any of His children hope to escape His discipline (Hebrews 12:7)?

3. What is the purpose of God's discipline on believers (Hebrews 12:10–11)?

4. What analogies are used to describe a believer who does not respond well to God's discipline (Hebrews 12:12–13)?

5. What word in Hebrews 12:15 sums up the wrong response to discipline?

Thought

We should never diminish in our minds the dangerous nature of the discipline of God. It is a fearful thing to experience God's displeasure. What we can do is take heart in knowing that whatever God has allowed in our lives will work for our good in conforming us to the image of Christ (Romans 8:28–29). We are called unto eternal glory by Christ Jesus, but we may have to suffer a while so that we can be established, strengthened, and settled. The right response, then, is to humble ourselves under the mighty hand of God (1 Peter 5:6, 10).

CHAPTER SEVEN

A TALE THAT IS TOLD

...we spend our years as a tale that is told.—PSALM 90:9

"We spend our years as a tale that is told." No truer words have ever been spoken.

Our lives on earth are like a short story—a brief introduction followed by a few pages filled with a mixture of intrigue, monotony, happiness, and horror. It's a page turner until quickly, before the plotlines are fully developed and resolved, an abrupt conclusion. In the scope of eternity, our brief history on earth—and all the events entailed in it—can be expressed in a thought. In the end, an abbreviated inscription on a tombstone will sum it all up as a name accompanied by the date of birth and the date of death.

I'll never forget the day in my ministry when I was called to the hospital to support a young couple who was about to have their first baby. On the same day, I was called to be present with a lady who had lost her father. She gave me the name of a funeral home a few towns away. Amazingly, both the hospital and the funeral home were in the same city, and both were located on the same street just a block apart.

Since the funeral home viewing hours were extended, I decided to go to the hospital first. I talked with the young woman in labor. I prayed with her and her husband for about fifteen minutes and then excused myself. I told them that I would return later not knowing how long it would take for the baby to come.

As I was walking down the hall, I saw a nurse spring to her feet and swiftly walk past me. I did not think much of it at the time, but later I learned that she was heading to the room I just left. The baby arrived a few moments later.

I walked out of the bright hospital lobby, down the sidewalk, and into the funeral home doors looking for the grieving family that needed my support. What a different atmosphere than the one I had just left! I walked out of the light and into the dark. I left a place of anticipation and entered a place of plaintive sorrow. I left a place of gain and entered a place of loss.

My pastoral protocol was obvious and plain. I prayed with the relatives who were looking at the lifeless form of the loved one in the casket. I hugged each one and expressed my sympathy. I stayed as long as I was needed. I sat in silence, praying. Others came. The room grew full.

Eventually, I sensed that my ministry at the funeral home was fulfilled for the time being. In the space of an hour and a half, I was back at the hospital—this time in the nursery holding a new baby girl.

What an amazing day! By God's grace, I was afforded the life-changing encounter of witnessing life's beginning and life's end in one afternoon.

There was something emblematic about that experience. It's a recorded message which has been played over and over and remained vivid in my mind and heart since. The brightness of birth is soon followed by the darkness of death. As it relates to time and space, the two are only a few short steps away.

As I have been writing this book, I have witnessed the deaths of two men related to our church. One man I did not know personally. His wife has been attending our church for a few weeks. I was with her as she went to the morgue to see the body of her husband who had died the night before. This man, who previously was strong and healthy, had wasted away to skin and bones because of cancer. The other man was faithful in our church. He too had cancer. This man had endured many hard treatments and close calls. When I arrived, he was awake and aware. We had sweet fellowship together, but something inside me said that probably this was the last time I would see him alive. I think that something inside him revealed the same thing as he hugged me and cried expressing his love for me as his pastor and friend. Sadly, we were both right.

There is no way to leave these experiences without being reminded of my own mortality. I feel as if I'm living on borrowed time. God could take me home at any moment. As a cancer patient, I looked at the faces of these two men and saw myself.

The first gentleman died of a type of cancer similar to mine. As I viewed his dead body in his void visage, I saw my future. The other gentleman was so vibrant just a few short days before. His eyes were full of gracious compassion and faith. His smile would light up a room. In a series of short moments, all this was taken from him. As I considered this I said to myself, "Is this how it will be for me?" The funeral was a few days later. I was honored to officiate such a blessed event.

At the service, one by one, family and friends stood behind the pulpit to talk about what a blessing he was. The memorial lasted for an hour, but it seemed to pass so quickly. In no time those in attendance had either gone their way or were still standing in the fellowship hall drinking punch, eating crackers and cookies, or looking at a picture montage displayed in the room. All were trying desperately to hold on to the slight opportunity to reminisce with close relations and acquaintances from far and near. Those of the present generation will remember. Some will struggle to remember more than others. In time, the young ones' memories of that day will fade. They will rehearse scenes in their minds only when they see a picture of some vaguely familiar form—familiar enough to stir some obscurely-stored memory. The next generation will know only what they've been told. Soon, no one on earth will know anything substantial about this man's amazing life.

It's hard to face the facts about the obscure nature of life on earth.

I recall hearing a preacher talk about an epitaph on a European monastery grave marker. It read, "Remember friends as you walk by, as you are now so once was I. As I am now, you will shortly be. Prepare thyself to follow me." This can be a depressing thought, but it does not have to be. The temporal nature of earthly life can be a motivation to use each moment in the best possible manner for Christ. The brevity of life breeds a greater interest and investment in eternity beyond the grave. The gloom of passing days can turn to glory if you think about what can happen by investing your time on earth wisely.

In verse 9 of our psalm, Moses is making a turn. His perspective is changing from darkness to light, from gloom to glory. The same can happen to us when on the detours of life, we acknowledge that life has a dark side.

There are limitations to our existence on earth. We must understand that fact clearly. It is only then that we can view the light of each new day in the full brilliance displayed by the mercies of God—which are new every morning. While we are still alive, we have hope for a productive future. If we are not dead, we are still breathing so that we can find some blessing in the will of God for the present. Even when life is soured by sin and suffering, we can look to God for a mitigating measure of favor. Even when we are off the select course, we can still count on God to light the next step in our journey. Wisdom is there for the asking if we will simply apply our hearts to it.

EXTRA POINTS TO PONDER

Questions

1. How does Psalm 78:39 describe our lives on earth?

2. How does 1 Chronicles 29:15 describe the same?

3. What perishes with the wicked, unbelieving man when his life is over (Proverbs 11:7)?

4. What else do they lose? And what is forgotten about them (Ecclesiastes 9:5)?

5. What is said of the righteous after they die (Psalm 112:6)?

Thought

Compared to eternity, our lives on earth are but a short blip in time. Our days are being spent quickly. The older we get the more aware we become of this fact. This by itself is a grievous thought. But because our lives are hidden with Christ in God, as believers, we can be assured that our short existence on earth is not vain or wasted. Every moment contains promise in that we can use it for that which is eternally recognized and rewarded. We are spending our lives, yes; but we can also invest them in that which is everlasting.

CHAPTER EIGHT

TEACH US TO NUMBER OUR DAYS

The days of our years are threescore years and ten; and if by reason of strength they be fourscore years, yet is their strength labour and sorrow; for it is soon cut off, and we fly away. Who knoweth the power of thine anger? even according to thy fear, so is thy wrath. So teach us to number our days...—PSALM 90:10–12

The psalmist prayed in Psalm 39:4, "Lord, make me to know mine end, and the measure of my days, what it is; that I may know how frail I am." Moses concurs with his fellow psalmist when he says, "Teach us to number our days."

What did both of these writers mean by their prayers to God? How do we know the measure of our days? How do we number our days?

One thing is certain: these verses call on us to consider the brevity of this life on earth. We are compelled to consider the current point in our individual lives compared to the average and standard life expectancy of mankind. This practice helps us as we break life down into small increments and come to realize that every day is a gift from God.

I heard a missionary recommend in a sermon that we use a typical yardstick to help us with the task of numbering our days. One end of the stick represents birth, while the other end represents the average human life of seventy years and death. Then he said that it is sobering to mark a line on the place representing your age at the moment. For me, forty-eight years old would be at about the twenty-four-inch mark.

From the looks of it, I am about twelve inches away from death. Well, not really, but almost two thirds of my life is over if I live to be seventy.

Wow! What a revelation! I am not going to be around here for long. If I'm going to serve the Lord and lay up treasure in Heaven, I'd better do it while I have the time and energy.

These verses tell me that my energy is fading fast. My body is breaking down. Moses' admonition here is that should God choose to extend my life, and somehow by reason of strength I live to the ripe old age of eighty, I have no reason for pride in that extra strength. Those added years will be full of labored activity and the sorrow that comes with it. Instead of boasting of potential life ahead I should be saying with the anonymous psalmist in Psalm 102:11 that my days are like a declining shadow. Old age is a time of increasing aches, pains, declining vigor, and loss.

Solomon aptly and poetically describes the pains of agedness in Ecclesiastes 12. Speaking to young people, Solomon, the preacher, describes what is coming to all of us in our latter years. In verse 1, he calls these years "evil days"—not evil in the moral sense but in the sense of being unfavorable and hard. Then, he goes on to describe the physical effects of the declining years. In verse 2, he says that the sun, moon, and stars will be darkened, speaking of the diminished vitality of the twilight years. In the same verse, he adds that the clouds will not return after the rain. In old age, vigor fades and is lost, never being renewed to the same degree. Solomon goes on in verses 3–5 to describe symbolically the weakening of the arms and legs, the dimming of the eyes, teeth falling out, the loss of sleep, increased phobias, gray hair, a halted gait, and loss of sexual interest.

Great! We middle-agers have a lot to look forward to, don't we?

If that is not enough to depress us, Solomon closes this passage by comparing death to the breaking of a golden bowl when it is cut from the silver chord holding it in its decorative setting and a pitcher falling down, shattering as the wheel on the well breaks under the weight of drawn water (Ecclesiastes 12:6). In modern parlance, we are all going down with a crash! Speaking in similar terms, Moses says that even if we live longer than expected, we are "soon cut off." (At least, he adds that we "fly away" instead of falling to the ground in pieces. For that reason, I prefer Moses' picture rather than the former.)

What are we to do with these thoughts? Are we to dwell on the darkness ahead? That can't help us. Are we to spend our days pining for a do-over? That's not profitable, either.

When we are on a different way than we wished for or expected, we have no time for deleterious dread or useless regret. Unless we are at the end of the yardstick, there is still time ahead. But since that time is ticking away fast, we had better use it wisely. There is no making up for the past, but there is such a thing as making use of the present. That is what it means to number our days.

As stated previously, Moses is seeing death all around due to the awful wrath and discipline of God. So he tells us to number our days—not only because the typical life span is brief, but also because God, in wrath, may take us home sooner.

Who knows the power of God's anger? Moses says that the fear of God, by man, should rise in regard to it.

God's wrath is more awful than our greatest conception of it; therefore, God is due the highest possible measure of fear and reverential regard. The same God who spoke the world into existence can destroy it. He showed this power once by bringing a world-wide flood in which only eight souls were saved. The Flood is just a small example of the power of His displeasure. Although a rainbow reminds us that He will never exercise His wrath in this way again, we should not be led to believe that we are safe from His judgment altogether. We are not. Therefore, with the real threat of His displeasure, we must make full use of each day in line with His favor and blessing.

Once again, you may think that this is Old Testament language only, but, as I stated previously, even John in the New Testament warns Christians that "there is a sin unto death" (1 John 5:16). God will not let us, as believers, stay in sin without discipline. He will convict us to correct us. He will chastise us to correct us. And if those methods prove insufficient, He may even take us home early to correct us fully and finally. God will ensure our ultimate sanctification even if it takes an untimely death to do so.

"But the Christian is no longer under condemnation!" you may protest, citing Romans 8:1.

Many love to cite this verse in the contemporary age of distorted grace and soft Christianity, but this verse does not mean that God's people avoid temporal judgment—only eternal judgment. It is true that, in Christ, we have no need to fear the eternal judgment of God for sin. Christ, in His own body, bore God's wrath on the cross. This glorious reality should compel us to lifelong love-driven service for God (2 Corinthians 5:14). This, however, is only one side of the coin. In Christ, we are exempt the eternal judgment of God, but we are not exempt the parental discipline of God. The Apostle Paul, who under the inspiration of the Holy Spirit penned the "no condemnation" found in the book of Romans, also wrote to the Christians at Corinth warning them that if they continued to disregard the Lord's Supper, they could expect God's discipline unto death. He said in 1 Corinthians 11:30,

"For this cause many are weak and sickly among you, and many sleep." Then he adds, "For if we would judge ourselves, we should not be judged" (verse 31). If many in that day were said to be dead due to corrective discipline, we are left to wonder how many today are dangerously close to that same judgment.

Moses told the people of Israel to number their days because he knew that their days were numbered. In so doing, he is only reiterating that which he has been saying since verse 3.

I will not belabor this point much further. The final word here is that this accounting for life's brevity is leading us somewhere—specifically, to wisdom. In Ecclesiastes 7:2, Solomon tells us that we get more wisdom from attending a funeral than by going to a party. In Psalm 90, Moses accounts for the same. Numbering our days, he says, helps us to apply our hearts unto wisdom.

A lack of wisdom may have caused us to get off the perfect path in the first place, and it is the acquisition of wisdom that will help proceed from where we are with purpose and blessing. The "Plan B" prayer is a prayer for prudence to progress. So let's read further with that in mind.

EXTRA POINTS TO PONDER

Questions

1. How old was Caleb when he took Hebron (Joshua 14:10)?

2. How did he describe his health (Joshua 14:11)?

3. How did Job die (Job 42:17)?

4. How did God describe Abraham at the time of his death (Genesis 25:8)?

5. What blessing did God give Moses in his later years (Deuteronomy 34:7)?

Thought

Old age does not have to be a complete burden. The verses on Psalm 90:10–12 give us hope that, if God chooses, He can bless us with extra strength and ability to do whatever He has called us to do late in life. In an act of mercy, He can even extend our lives and ministries on earth. That being said, God's mercy in this way is no guarantee. The only day that we are assured of is today. Counting our days is not looking ahead as much as it is taking full advantage of that which is present—the here and now.

CHAPTER NINE

APPLYING OUR HEARTS TO WISDOM

...that we may apply our hearts unto wisdom.
—Psalm 90:12

If we are going to apply our hearts to something, we have to know what it is. Moses prayed for wisdom with the urgency of knowing that his days were numbered, and he desired to apply his heart to it.

But what *is* wisdom?

The proposed definitions of wisdom you may read are as wide and varied as the number of Bible expositors who state them. Wading through all the words on wisdom is a challenge, but I have found that the general consensus is, in short, that wisdom is the application of God's revelation. It goes beyond the mere knowledge of the Word of God and relates to a godly perspective that is put into practice.

While I'm at it, let me do some expounding myself and add some more words to the mix.

We may be smart. We may have a lot of know-how, but the circumstances of life should inevitably cause us to realize that we need a resource beyond ourselves. Sooner or later, we rise to the limits of our intellect and discover our own incompetence. Those who never experience this discovery are dangerously deluded, spiritually dull, or worse, dead.

We live with a desperate need of God's wisdom, and in a way, wisdom starts with that recognition.

Proverbs 9:10 says, "The fear of the Lord is the beginning of wisdom." In other words, wisdom starts with God; it is derived from a reverential relationship with Him. To be wise, one has to have a keen awareness of God. By His Word, one must believe that Jehovah God is the creator of the universe, that He has revealed absolute truth about Himself and how to live, and that established moral and practical precepts, principles, and values flow from this revelation.

Wisdom is not "book smarts." There is such a person as an educated fool.

Wisdom is not street smarts or common sense. It is divine perspective applied to the situations and complexities of life.

In the eighth chapter of Proverbs, Solomon presents an amazing list of wisdom's attributes. Consider the attractive quality of wisdom in light of these traits:

- Wisdom is *available*—"Doth not wisdom cry?...She crieth at the gates..." (vv. 1, 3).
- Wisdom is *truthful*—"Hear...For my mouth shall speak truth..." (vv. 6–7).
- Wisdom is *understandable*—"All the words...are plain to him that understandeth..." (vv. 8–9).
- Wisdom is *valuable*—"For wisdom is better than rubies..." (v. 11).
- Wisdom is *practical*—"I wisdom...find out knowledge of witty inventions" (v. 12).
- Wisdom is *powerful*—"I am understanding; I have strength" (v. 14).
- Wisdom is *effectual*—"By me kings reign..." (v. 15).
- Wisdom is *personal*—"I love them that love me..." (v. 17).
- Wisdom is *fruitful*—"My fruit is better than gold..." (v. 19).
- Wisdom is *spiritual*—"I lead in the way of righteousness..." (v. 20).
- Wisdom is *eternal*—"The Lord possessed me...before his works of old" (v. 22).
- Wisdom is *continual*—"Blessed is the man...watching daily at my gates..." (v. 34).
- Wisdom is *critical*—"But he that sinneth against me wrongeth his own soul..." (v. 36).
- Because of all this, wisdom is *wonderful!*

No wonder that Solomon says to us that "wisdom is the principal thing"; therefore, we need to "get wisdom" (Proverbs 4:7). Wisdom is the essential element of godly living.

But how do we get it?

Our passage says that we get wisdom by applying our hearts to it. Proverbs 2 tells us that we have to incline our ears unto it (verse 2), passionately cry out for it (verse 3), and seek for it as if searching for hidden treasure (verse 4). Verse 6 says that God gives wisdom. James 1:5 adds that if we lack wisdom, we can ask for it from God and know that He gives it liberally. He gives it generously and, in King James English, "upbraideth not."

I like that part.

When it says that God "upbraideth not," it means that God gives wisdom without reproach.

God will not insult or mock the person who prays for wisdom as if to say, "You dummy, don't you know enough to know this yourself," or "Don't you know better?" God will not say with a smirk, "Are you coming to Me again?" He does not gather the angels around and say, "Would you look at this idiot? He just doesn't get it!" On the contrary, God loves to give us wisdom. It just takes an impassioned plea in prayer and a diligent pursuit in devotional Bible study to take advantage of His benevolence.

So wisdom is available; it's just not automatic.

Again in the book of James, when God speaks of giving wisdom to those who ask, He adds, "But let him ask in faith, nothing wavering. For he that wavereth is like a wave of the sea driven with the wind and tossed. For let not that man think that he shall receive any thing…" (James 1:6, 7). God is saying, through the writer James, that He supplies wisdom only to those who ask and seek in faith. Faith is fostered by the Word, and our prayer for wisdom must flow from time spent in the Bible. Wisdom is the application of God's Word to the situation at hand. So we must start at the revelation we have in our hands—the Scriptures.

The wavering person does not put in the devotional time that wisdom requires. So, he asks for wisdom without faith. He just wants instant instruction without diligent effort. He wants a quick fix. He is like a wave, James says—up and down with God, not really sure if God is trustworthy and if His Word is right. He is not single-minded in seeking God's will. He wants comfort and convenience, not truth. He wants God's way only if it fits with his way. He is coming to God, yes, but not in a way that expresses he is completely convinced that God's way is best. To this person, prayer is a formality. It is something you try. It's like throwing something up to the ceiling to see if it sticks. It is not a privilege to him. It is not a necessity, nor is it a means to know God and commune closely with Him. And he prays, but he prays amiss, and receives zilch…nada…nothing.

The person who applies his heart to wisdom has a different spirit.

The person who applies his heart to wisdom has already spent serious time in Bible study when he prays. He prioritizes his prayers in light of the revelation of God's Word. Instead of asking merely for deliverance or healing or help, he asks for wisdom. He knows that he needs wisdom first and foremost.

After all, what good is deliverance if you don't have wisdom to use your newly found freedom well? What good is healing if your health is wasted on unwise pursuits? What good is God's help if you waste an opportunity for growth?

Wisdom allows us to see beyond our trials to the results God is trying to achieve. When we sincerely seek wisdom, we are not so much asking for the removal of challenges but for the right approach to them and the ability to navigate in their midst. In the end with wisdom, we understand that God's deliverance comes in the trial as well as through it.

This was the perspective that Moses espoused in Psalm 90. Moses needed wisdom as he went back into the wilderness.

Also, it is wisdom that marks our path through unchartered places on the roundabout routes of our lives. No matter where we are and no matter how far off we are from the ideal, with wisdom we can proceed with hope and confidence. Even though the way ahead seems tough, if we apply our hearts, God will show us where to find an oasis of mercy. God will give us a measure of blessing that, if not for the fact that we experience it firsthand, we would otherwise think it impossible.

EXTRA POINTS TO PONDER

Questions

1. What action verbs do you find in Proverbs 2:1–4 that describe our quest for wisdom?

2. According to verse 5 of the same passage, what can we expect if we do take these actions?

3. Describe the actions of the fools who do not engage in the pursuit of wisdom (Proverbs 1:20–25).

4. What can these people expect (Proverbs 1:26–32)?

5. Proverbs 3:13 tells us that we will be happy when we find and get wisdom. What kind of happiness do you think wisdom brings?

Thought

Wisdom is only for those who put in the diligent work to search it out in God's Word and who sincerely pray to get it. God does not bless the indolent individual with this blessing. When we, by the circumstances of life, become aware of our mortality, we have a prime opportunity to break free from foolishness to pursue wisdom with urgency. And God will help us to come to this perspective. That is why we must pray, "Teach us to number our days." In fact, since we need wisdom today, what's stopping us from praying that prayer now?

CHAPTER TEN

HOW LONG?

Return, O LORD, how long? And let it repent thee concerning thy servants.—PSALM 90:13

"How long will this last?"

"When will the restriction end?" "When will this round of discipline be over?"

"God, am I done for?"

"If not, when will the blessings kick in again?"

Have your prayers ever sounded like that?

Moses is praying for God's demeanor to change toward himself and the nation. He prays for God to turn toward them with favor. He prays for a change with a question on his lips, "How long?"

No one wants to endure a trial of affliction, but if it must be, it is a normal thing to ask God how long it will last.

David asked this question again and again in his psalms.

In Psalm 6, he asked God how long his soul will be vexed.

In Psalm 13, David felt as if God had hidden His face from him, and David asked, "How long?" In fact in the space of two verses, four times he asked "How long?"

In Psalm 94:3 he asked God, "…how long shall the wicked triumph?"

And the list goes on.

Who said that God's way for us would be easy? It's not an easy road. Our faults and failures make it more difficult. We live in a sin-cursed world, and the consequences of our own choices and the choices of those around us make for some long, hard journeys. No one in the service of God enjoys the desert path of God's discipline whether it is of their own doing or as a byproduct of the failure of those around them. These desert trips are usually not short. In fact, many side roads off the "interstate of the ideal" go on for miles.

You know the feeling. You and your family are on the way to your favorite vacation spot. You're moving. You're making tracks. Then suddenly, the traffic is diverted and you're headed down a narrow road in another direction. Your GPS recalculates every thirty seconds, and your ETA changes with it. Everyone in the car gets cranky. The kids in the back start the chorus: "How long 'til we get there, Daddy? How long?"

There is no way that you can wiggle your nose or wave a wand and get where you want to be. That is out of the question.

The question that comes to mind is this: Is there anything to see, do, and enjoy on the way that you have been forced to take? You can't change the situation. You can only make the most of it.

Often, great scenery is abundant along the side roads. Some of the best diners are off the beaten path. Some of the most memorable moments and family bonding opportunities happen when the trip takes an unplanned turn.

As we continue in Psalm 90, we sense that this perceptibly pessimistic psalm is turning a positive direction.

"How so," you ask?

Well, Moses would not even pray this prayer unless he believed that somehow his petitions could influence God and attract His favor. Moses believed in the prevailing goodness of God. Moses believed that prayer works. He believed that "all things work together for good" before the phrase was ever written. Here, by God's grace, he was able to look for the silver lining.

One technical side note before we find that lining with him: Some biblical scholars bemoan the use of the word "repent" here in relation to God. I understand their concern. The prevailing modern understanding of repentance is that of sorrow in a moral sense, the regret of sin, etc. Obviously, God does not repent in that way. In fact, He says that He does not repent as a man. But that is not to say that He does not repent in any other sense (1 Samuel 15:11, 15:29). To say that one repents can simply suggest a change in that person's sentiment from pleasure to sorrow. The word is used, in general, to express a change in demeanor resulting in a change of direction. Some prefer the word "relent" in most passages that relate to God in this way. To say that God relents is to give the impression that God "gives in" to man. I do not know if that is the appropriate perception we want to give about God. In my mind, the word "repent" is just as proper, if not preferred.

In any case, the question remains: does God change in response to man in time? And if He does, how does this affect our understanding of His immutability?

If it is said that God never changes, can we without a doubt say that He changes His thoughts, intents, or course in time? Didn't God say to Malachi, "…I am the Lord, I change not…" (Malachi 3:6)?

Let's see if we can resolve this paradox.

God feels emotion, including sorrow. Since emotions flow from thoughts and are interconnected, if God's emotions change to feel sorrow, He must also be thinking differently. His emotions are prompted by a change of thought and can result in a change of intent or action. In my opinion, to deny or to attribute this form of repentance or altered sentiment to a mere anthropomorphic expression makes God look static and unfeeling. And when the context dictates that God repented in the sense of changing His demeanor and projected or professed course of action, it does not diminish His immutability in the least.

Immutability speaks of the fact that God's character never changes. His attributes do not change. He never grows or develops. It does not mean that God's thoughts are not altered based on the conditions of men and conditions on the earth or that He cannot respond emotionally or willfully to man in time.

The fact that He foreknows what He will do does not change the reality that in time He must do what He must do. At times, He acts in ways that vary, based on His response to man. He deals with men in a dynamic not a static way. When in passages He says that He was saddened by a situation, that is real. When it says that He thought to do something and did not, it means that His intent was redirected due to real conditions on the earth. Somehow His sovereign plan outside of time involves this redirection and allows Him to act in real time. As I stated earlier, I do not have to reconcile that for faith. I just read my Bible, and I know it is true.

(We do not have to understand everything in order to have faith. Instead, it is by faith that we come to a greater degree of understanding than we would otherwise reach through our reasoning power. As Hebrews 11:3 says, "Through faith we understand that the worlds were framed by the word of God…." The origin of the universe would be senseless in any other way.)

Back to the issue of God repenting…

God works in two dimensions, in time and outside of it. Some passages emphasize one dimension of God's work, while some emphasize the other dimension. This is a mystery, but it has to be true. Otherwise God's actions in time are not real and relational but set, static, and somehow superficial. God won't let us think that. Instead, He lets us know that our prayers and behaviors influence His emotional state and course of action. When we make God's repentance an anthropomorphic accommodation or mere anthropopathy, we are denying His relational and time-oriented work and ways.

There is a Bible balance to be found, and it is somewhere between static sovereignty and open theism.

Enough said on that topic. Let's move on.

The important thing for us to see is that Moses prayed for God to give blessing in the midst of this trial. He did so because He believed that God is inclined to answer prayer and that being blessed is possible no matter the situation. You and I have to believe the same. Otherwise, why go forward on our detour or from wherever we are at the moment? Why even make a move if there is only a spiritual wasteland ahead? Let's just end our lives and get to Heaven as quickly as possible.

We know that we cannot do that.

Let's do what Moses did. Let's pray for and believe in a blessing.

Look at other passages which say of God that He changed His intent and course in time by diminishing His judgment.

Exodus 32:11–13 says Moses interceded for the nation of Israel when God expressed His intent to destroy them. In response to his prayer, God did not.

In Jonah 3, we read that Jonah was told to declare to the people of Nineveh that God would destroy their city in forty days (verse 4). Much to Jonah's chagrin, they repented and turned from their evil ways. God in turn changed His professed and projected judgment and spared them (verse 10).

In one of my favorite passages, Hezekiah prayed that God would change His disposition toward him. In 2 Kings 20:1–6, we find Isaiah telling Hezekiah to get his house in order because he would soon die. Hezekiah pleaded with the Lord to have mercy on him, and God not only spared his life, but amazingly declared, "…I will add unto thy days fifteen years…" (verse 6). Why do I love this passage so much? Ever since I was diagnosed with cancer I have prayed consistently, "Lord, please have mercy on me and extend my life and ministry."

So far, so good.

In considering what Moses is saying in Psalm 90:13, we are led to a similar example found in Joel 2:12–14. In the previous passages, God had pronounced His judgment on the people of Judah. But Joel the prophet tells the people to repent and turn unto the Lord believing that even in the midst of judgment He is gracious. In Joel 2:14, he ends by saying to the people, "Who knoweth if he will return and repent, and leave a blessing behind Him…." Joel said that God may just turn in grace, change His intent, and reserve a blessing for us.

The Spirit-led prayer recorded in Joel 2:14 gives us a great understanding of God's response to man and work in time. It says that God does not have to do what we ask just because we ask. That's why Joel says (paraphrased), "Repent, pray, and let's see what happens—who knows?" This prayer also encourages us with the fact that God can defer to His people, considering their prayers, and alter His plan in time.

I speak like Joel to God's people all the time—not in the same words but in a similar fashion. Personally, I have found that the essence of my pastoral ministry is to take people where they are with all of the complications in their lives and give them hope in God's gracious work for the future. I work with them to go forward from a particular point on the map that marks their place in the permissive will of God. My advice is always, "Let's confess our sins, deal with the reality of our situation, pray, and see what God does from here."

I have never met a Christian who does not have to work through some issue of human failure. Maybe there is a church full of perfect people always living in God's perfect will, but I would suspect that, if that were true, they would not need a pastor. And, if they did desire one, they certainly would not want an imperfect pastor like me.

No one is exempt from the biblical description of the human condition, "All we like sheep have gone astray..." (Isaiah 53:6).

All that to say, whenever we find ourselves falling short of the ideal of God's perfect will, we can still trust God for a measure of blessing. We may not escape an inevitable consequence that comes our way, but no matter how long it must be that we face it, we still can pray for hope, relief, change, and new joy.

EXTRA POINTS TO PONDER

Questions

Read 2 Samuel 12:9–25.

1. What were David's sins that kept him from God's perfect will in his family life (verse 9)?

2. What consequences would come to him (verses 11, 12, and 14)?

3. After David repented, did God forgive David (verse 13)?

4. After what Nathan told David, why did David pray for his child (verses 16 and 22)?

5. God did not spare the child, but what blessing did He allow (verse 24), and how long did it take to come?

6. What does the last phrase in verse 24 say about God?

Thought

David's situation may be an extreme case, but, as with Moses, on a detour of discipline and trial, he believed in God for grace and blessing. To stay encouraged in the midst of our detours we must believe and pray for the same. God is just. He has to let the consequences of sin take their courses. At the same time, He is merciful and responds to His people with help, hope, healing, and deliverance. Those who believe in God's mercy pray for it. Those who pray for it are blessed.

CHAPTER ELEVEN

EARLY MERCY

O satisfy us early with thy mercy; that we may rejoice and be glad all our days.—Psalm 90:14

This verse is the essence of the "Plan B" prayer.

When things go south and the ideal is out of reach, we need to pray as soon as possible for a measure of mercy. If we are off the preferred path, we need a token of grace. What we need is a map. We need a purpose—something to live for. If we are broken down and empty, we need a fill-up of gladness that will fuel our faith until the end. And since there is not much time left on our journey, if we are going to get what we require, we need to get it early.

Moses knew where to go in his day of desperation. In verse 14 of our psalm, he prays for a satisfying source of

God's mercy—some respite from the harsh conditions, some supernatural sympathy to soften the coming blow. Without trying to be presumptuous, he asked that God would be gracious enough to do this right away.

In our condition away from Canaan, we all need early mercy! Like Moses, we can and should pray for it. The question is, can we count on God to come through?

Let's look to other characters in the Bible and find out.

Speaking of early mercy, think of what Adam and Eve needed when they walked from the gates of Eden never to return.

Genesis 3 ends with God driving Adam and Eve out of Eden while setting an angelic sentinel to guard against their re-entry. Behind these two newly-corrupted people was a plush paradise of fruit trees with multi-colored blooms. Behind them was a perfect atmosphere at just the right temperature, not too hot, not too cool. Behind them was a flawless place, a glorious garden habitat. Eden—what a sublime spot it was! What a tragedy to be driven away!

Adam and Eve lived in pure innocence in Eden. There was no guilt. They walked with God. They talked to Him daily. They had no fear. They worked with blissful oneness and tended to the plants and trees. They knew nothing but love in Eden.

Adam and Eve had to walk away from Eden. Because of profound failure, they were forced to leave. They walked away, heads lowered.

We can imagine that as they plodded on they must have stopped at some point, looked at each other in bewilderment, and said, "Now what? Now where do we go? What do we do now?"

Now was the time for their first prayer. It was a "Plan B" prayer. In Eden, they talked to God directly, in person. But the day they walked away, things were not the same. They had to pray. They had to cry out to God from afar. What would they say? What did they say? No one knows. In all likelihood, their first prayer was nothing more than a request for early mercy.

The writer of Genesis does not tell us in detail what happened as they walked out into a cruel, cursed world. Somehow they settled, found means of survival, made a home, and started to make a living. Who gave them the means to survive? God did. And God did much more than that. He blessed them greatly.

Genesis 4 starts by saying, "And Adam knew Eve his wife; and she conceived, and bare Cain, and said, I have gotten a man from the Lord." Soon Abel came along. In time, more children were added. God was merciful and blessed them with a family. There would be hardships and heartbreaks to follow. But with these also came adventure, felicity, and joy.

This initial example shows that God is in the practice of doling out mercy.

Jacob learned about God's merciful ways.

Remember Jacob? His name meant "deceiver." He was the guy who tricked his brother Esau and defrauded his father Isaac to secure the firstborn's blessing and inheritance.

Ultimately, God indeed intended for Jacob to receive this cherished benefit, but not in this way.

Because of Jacob's deceptive ways, God could have easily said to Jacob, "That's it. You're on your own!" But He did not. God spared his life and secured his ultimate safety. Esau was ready to kill Jacob, but at a fortuitous time, God allowed him the opportunity to flee from the threat of his brother and make his way into the wilderness to the safe settlement of his uncle Laban. (You can read the whole account in Genesis 27.)

In the desert, Jacob and his clan moved onward, stopping to rest at times and sleeping on the hard ground. On one of these occasions while sleeping at the Hard Rock Hotel, God met with Jacob in a special way saying to him, "...The land whereon thou liest, to thee will I give it, and to thy seed" (Genesis 28:13). This merciful revelation showed Jacob that not only would he survive, but also that he and his family would thrive in this foreign place. And he did. He lived on. He made it through. His family grew to become a great nation.

God gave Jacob early mercy as he went forward. This mercy was the means by which He used to change this young man's character. In the process of time, he even changed Jacob's name to "Israel" meaning "prince with God" to reflect his transformed heart and new standing. The nation that came from him was called Israel as well, and by God's indomitable and prevailing goodness, they live in the land of promise today.

Another great example of early mercy is found in 2 Samuel 12. In this passage we read that David's sin of killing Uriah and taking his wife Bathsheba to be his was revealed by

God to the prophet Nathan. Nathan, in turn, told David all the consequences that would come because of his fateful decision to please himself and do these awful acts. The outcome? David's newborn child, born by Bathsheba, would die (12:14) and his family would be marked by violence following his example (12:10–12).

According to Nathan's word, the baby became sick. With plaintive passion, David began to fast and pray for God to spare the innocent child. He prayed all night. Begging for clemency to escape this painful penalty, he agonized in prayer. But God did not do as he asked. Even after seven days of pleading, the baby died as foretold.

What followed is as perplexing as it is poignant.

In an amazing act of resiliency after David heard the tragic news, he wiped his tears and went on with life. He ceased his prayers, washed his face, ate his breakfast, and started a new day with purpose. This was a shock to those who witnessed it and those who read it.

What? How could he do that? How could his grief be so short-lived?

His servants could not believe David's response. They boldly remarked to him, "Why aren't you still mourning?" (my paraphrase of verse 21). David made an astounding statement when he replied, "...While the child was yet alive, I fasted and wept: for I said, Who can tell whether God will be gracious to me, that the child may live? But now he is dead, wherefore should I fast? can I bring him back again? I shall go to him, but he shall not return to me" (vv. 22–23).

"Aha!" you may say. "God was not merciful to David."

But wait! Mercy was coming, and it came quickly.

Don't stop reading.

Verse 24 of 2 Samuel 12 says, "And David comforted Bathsheba his wife, and went in unto her, and lay with her: and she bare a son, and he called his name Solomon: and the LORD loved him."

Talk about early mercy! David and Bathsheba's first child had just passed away, and God worked to give them a new child, an heir, a son. Not only that, but this son would be the next king whom God would love enough to give the greatest measure of wisdom ever known to man. Because of God's gracious bestowal of understanding, Solomon was said to be the wisest man who ever lived. And if that were not enough, he would also be included in the line of Christ.

Don't tell me God is not gracious and merciful! He was, and He is still today.

God made a way for Adam and Eve, Jacob, David, and countless others down through time. When we are on our detoured direction, we have to find the faith to believe God in mercy will make a way for us. With Jeremiah, our firm conviction about God should be, "It is of the LORD's mercies that we are not consumed, because his compassions fail not. They are new every morning: great is thy faithfulness" (Lamentations 3:22–23).

If we truly believe in the goodness of God, our first prayer in times of difficulty should be a prayer for mercy. When facing God's discipline, we can still pray for mercy. Why shouldn't we? Mercy, by definition, is God's benevolent kindness toward the underserving. It is for those with no credit. It is for those who have lost their way.

Predominantly, Scripture views mercy as God withholding a degree of divine punishment. It is the mitigating disposition of His righteous character that stays the full execution of His wrath. Mercy is the first instinct and inclination He has toward His people.

Jeremiah said as much when he stated about God in Lamentations 3:32–33, "But though he cause grief, yet will he have compassion according to the multitude of his mercies. For he doth not afflict willingly…."

Nehemiah concurred when he described God's mercy toward Israel. About Israel he said to God, "But they and our fathers…refused to obey, neither were mindful of thy wonders that thou didst among them…." Then he added, "…but thou art a God ready to pardon, gracious and merciful, slow to anger, and of great kindness…" (Nehemiah 9:16–17).

Micah sums up this truth as well, declaring unto God: "Who is a God like unto thee, that pardoneth iniquity, and passeth by the transgression of the remnant of his heritage? He retaineth not his anger for ever, because he delighteth in mercy" (Micah 7:18).

God does not afflict willingly or with preferential intent. God delights in mercy.

We, then, can count on God's mercy to make our walk in this world much smoother than it might have been without it. We may experience blessing beyond that which we ever thought possible. When our sins find us out, when our deeds breed difficulty, when the path ahead seems rough, we need to pray for mercy.

God's mercy is plenteous, rich, and everlasting. And what makes it more desirable than already described is this: Mercy does more than lighten the severity of chastisement. It makes room for grace. With mercy, God makes it possible for us to enjoy some benevolent goodness on what would otherwise be a cursed course to travel. Because God is merciful, we can expect the way to be easier and the load lighter than we might have anxiously imagined. Also we can expect to find some surprising endowments along the way.

It is the expectation of God's mercy and grace that prompts Moses to pray a seemingly ironic, and yet, genuine prayer. He prays to God, "Make us glad according to our afflicted days" (my paraphrase).

Now that's a prayer we don't hear too often.

That's a prayer that would make the "health-and-wealth" or "name-it-and-claim-it!" preachers cringe.

Yet, it is a biblical prayer.

Should we be praying the same today?

Is there really such a thing as gladness in affliction?

Is there really such a thing as "overcoming joy"?

Yes! And mercy makes it happen. Read on.

EXTRA POINTS TO PONDER

Questions

1. What aspect of God's mercy can we relate to at any time (Lamentations 3:22)?

2. Even in times of discipline, what is God's thought toward us (Jeremiah 29:10–11)?

3. What is the only thing preventing us from receiving God's merciful provision (Jeremiah 29:12–13)?

4. According to Psalm 145:14, who does the Lord uphold? Who does He raise up?

5. According to Psalm 145:18–19, to whom does the Lord draw close? What does He do for them?

6. No matter where we are in life, if we fear the Lord, what is our source of hope (Psalm 147:11)?

Thought

God is merciful. Even when we have failed or fallen, He is ready to bless us at a moment's notice. When we don't know what's ahead, we can always count on God's mercy to be available if we only reach out for it and ask. Moses' prayer in Psalm 90 is instructive because he had a vision of blessing even though he was living with less than the ideal. His hope was in the Lord's mercy. He found grace, and so can we.

CHAPTER TWELVE

JOY IN THE WILDERNESS

Make us glad according to the days wherein thou hast afflicted us, and the years wherein we have seen evil.
—PSALM 90:15

Some presumptuous preachers tell us that, as Christians, we should never accept adversity. We all should be healthy and wealthy, they say. Well, if that is true, Moses, once again, didn't get the memo.

Moses not only accepted his adversity, but he also anticipated and prayed for gladness "according to," or in conjunction with, it. As he stated in the previous verse, Moses wished to rejoice the rest of his days. Rejoicing is an expression of joy. Moses did not want to walk around in the wilderness without joy. And he did not have to.

The ability to have joy in affliction is one of the most sublime truths in Scripture. It is sad that so many Christians want to avoid affliction at any cost while accepting a mistaken and perverted message from the "masters of misapplication." "God would not want you sick," they say. "God would not want you to struggle." Many have ears that itch for such hollow homilies. It's easy to understand why. A sugar-coated, self-help style sermon is much easier to listen to than one that tells the hard truth of how to deal with hardship. I contend that there is no real gladness in denying reality—only a manufactured, man-made mirth that comes by telling oneself that all will be well when it may not.

At some time, we will all be forced to live with something that is less than ideal. That does not mean we cannot have joy. In fact, our joy may be deeper and more profound when it is birthed out of that which may at first seem detrimental.

The "health-and-wealth" preachers prey on our natural aversion to affliction. They prey on our instinctive sense of self-protection. It is only human that we want to escape any form of discomfort. (There are a few sadists out there, but they are generally out of their minds.) Most of us like the soft, easy life. Our ears are inclined, then, to those who tell us that we can have it all.

What's missing in this *message du jour* is that sin is a barrier to any blessing, and all affliction is allowed by God. Even when our affliction is not due to any sin in particular, God may be using it as a preventative measure or to prepare us for greater service. With this in mind, we can expect much tribulation in this world. Our cheer comes in that we know that Jesus has ultimately overcome the world (John 16:33).

As I was going through the year of cancer treatments, a well-meaning Christian friend of mine gave me reading material from a "Word of Faith" perspective.

"Word of Faith" is the more technical term for the "health-and-wealth" perspective. The type of faith promoted in the Word of Faith movement is a faith in words—in precise, positive declarations. It is a faith in faith itself. It is not a faith in God alone.

When Jesus was in the Garden of Gethsemane facing the prospect of death, He prayed, "Father, if it be possible, let this cup pass from me" (Matthew 26:39). It was not as if He did not think His Father was able. In His humanity, Jesus was asking if it was possible *according to the Father's plan* to do things another way. That's why in Luke 22:42 Jesus' prayer in the garden is expressed this way: "Father, if thou be willing, remove this cup from me." And then Jesus adds, "nevertheless not my will, but thine, be done." The Word of Faith preachers do not tell us to pray this way. The word "if" is anathema to them. We must assume God is willing. They say that we must name, claim, and declare what we desire. This is a distorted view of the biblical doctrine of prayer.

In my opinion, the Word of Faith proponents are not promoting an absolute dependence upon God and His purpose for our lives. Personally, I read the books given to me purely out of curiosity. Actually, I scanned them. I did not have to turn through many pages to get the main point. The subtle insinuation was that I should not accept my illness and pray it away. Of course, I do believe that God can and will heal according to His will. I did pray for complete healing. I prayed passionately and diligently, but God did not heal me. According to The Word of Faith writers who I was reading, I might not have had the faith necessary to be healed. Contrary to what they say, what I have come to believe is this: God gave me the faith to accept my adversity and find joy in it.

I think I am in good company. After Paul prayed three times for his "thorn in the flesh" to be removed, he accepted it. He said, "Most gladly therefore will I rather glory in my infirmities, that the power of Christ may rest upon me" (2 Corinthians 12:9). Then he added, "Therefore I take pleasure in infirmities" (verse 10). That is one of the most shocking and yet satisfactory statements in the Bible. Why? Well, what Paul is exemplifying is this: if joy is circumstantial, there is no way to have it consistently, but if joy is available from God any time and in adversity, we can know that whatever we face, we can face it gladly, yeah, most gladly! If, as with Paul's adversity, God is preventing sin, we can rejoice. If, as with Moses' adversity, God is punishing sin, we can accept that and rejoice as well.

We certainly will never get where we need to be spiritually if we view joy as an end in itself. Joy is not something to be attained. It is a fruit of the Spirit (Galatians 5:22). It is something that comes as a by-product of spiritual life from God. We confuse the issue when in a supposed search for joy, we yearn for a pleasant physical or emotional experience that can be caught and held. This occurs when we think thoughts like, "When I am healthy I will finally be happy" or "If I get that job or make that money, I will surely be happy" and, possibly, "If I could only marry her, she will give me joy." There is such a thing as circumstantial happiness, but when we imagine life in this way, we will always judge lasting joy to be elusive.

Confusion comes when we associate joy only with its exuberant and ecstatic state. This condition can be associated with joy, but joy is not defined by it. Pleasure is not joy, although joy can be pleasurable. Joy must be derived from a place deeper than physical senses. Otherwise, how could we "rejoice in the Lord alway" (Philippians 4:4)? We always would have to be feeling good. Joy goes deeper. It is a spiritual thing. In its essence, joy is a warm glow of gladness in the spirit that is perceived more subtly than any accompanied physical sensation. The psalmist expressed this perception well when he said, "In the multitude of my thoughts within me thy comforts delight my soul" (Psalm 94:19).

God is the source of joy. He is the one who puts gladness in our hearts (Psalm 4:7). He is the one who can restore the joy of our salvation (Psalm 51:12). Joy can only come from Him, and that's why Moses prayed to God, "Make us glad."

God is also the object of joy. In his affliction, David said, "…my soul shall be joyful in the Lord…" (Psalm 35:9). In His presence is "fullness of joy" (Psalm 16:11). Although we may have to wait until Heaven to experience this fullness perfectly, we do not have to wait to know it at all. As we draw closer to Christ and abide in His presence, this spiritual gladness is bound to break through and settle our otherwise fluctuating spirit.

I contend that since joy is a condition that comes from close communion with God, it can be accentuated by adversity, and that which holds a key to joy is anything that draws us closer to Him. Matthew 5:12 tells that we can "rejoice, and be exceeding glad…" when facing persecution. Romans 5:3 says we can "glory in tribulation." First Peter 1:6–8 says that even though we may for a season be "in heaviness through manifold temptations," we can know that the "trial of our faith" is "precious." And although we cannot see Christ we can rejoice in Him with "joy unspeakable and full of glory." Joy during a trial is unspeakable because it is impossible to express or explain. It is a profound peace in affliction that does not make sense in natural terms.

This is real spiritual living. This is genuine Christianity, not some empty expectation to always live with a loaded wallet, a perfect body, and a wide-mouthed, pearly, white smile. When the conditions of our lives are less than ideal, this kind of joy is what we pray for. And when we do, we will find that the joy of the Lord is our strength (Nehemiah 8:10).

EXTRA POINTS TO PONDER

Questions

1. According to Proverbs 14:13, the unbeliever can enjoy great times of mirth while a pervasive spirit of sorrow and affliction exists in their soul. Why is that so?

2. What is the opposite condition which can be experienced by the Christian (1 Thessalonians 1:6; 1 Peter 4:13, 14)?

3. The Macedonian Christians had joy during what kind of circumstance (2 Corinthians 8:2)?

4. James tells us to reckon what to be a source of joy (James 1:2)?

5. Jesus told His disciples that they would be sorrowful after His departure, but after that, their sorrow would turn to joy. From where would their joy come (John 16:19, 20; John 16:7; Galatians 5:22)?

6. God's discipline may not seem joyous, but according to Hebrews 12:11 it is. Why?

Thought

Christian joy is not based on the physical conditions of the moment. Instead, joy is derived from the Holy Spirit as He helps us to recognize spiritual realities in the midst of our circumstances no matter how challenging they are. So, have joy no matter what!

CHAPTER THIRTEEN

AN ESTABLISHED WORK

Let thy work appear unto thy servants, and thy glory unto their children. And let the beauty of the L*ORD our God be upon us: and establish thou the work of our hands upon us: yea, the work of our hands establish thou it.*—PSALM 90:16–17

By the end of this prayer, we are able to sense that Moses was stirred in his spirit by God to believe in God for a blessing as he led a faithless people into the wilderness. He ended his prayer with a sense of purpose.

What could that purpose possibly be?

Moses still had work to do—to unite the people, keep them encouraged, and train a future generation to take possession of the Promised Land. This was a great task worthy of Moses' best effort and most fervent passion. In so doing, he fully expected God to establish his work. He had faith to believe that God would once again show His glory and providential hand.

Moses was wise enough to know that God does not bless indolence. We would be wise to understand this as well, especially when the diverted routes that we take are fraught with difficulty. We have to believe in God's ultimate goodness and prayerfully work as if we anticipate its outworking in this life and the life to come. Though the way may be tough and trying, we can count on unique and special tokens of grace ahead. Something good from God is bound to come. Blessings may be just around the bend if we are willing to work.

Many of God's blessings in life come in proportion to our participation. They come on account of our labor, not in spite of it. A vision for God's glory without a plan for sacrificial and obedient effort is useless. Once again, God blesses work. No matter where we are in life, as long as we are breathing and live in a body that functions, we can find something productive to do. By the grace of God, we can go forward and face the challenges ahead with initiative, diligence, and hope.

We live in a culture that promotes the pipe dream of instant success. Bookstores carry shelves full of motivational books with titles such as *Five Easy Steps to Financial Success* and *How to be a Millionaire before Thirty*. Radio infomercials tell us we can make six figures working only five hours a week. There is always a glowing testimonial to let us believe that it is possible. Of course, these bold blurbs are always followed by rushed disclaimers like "Results may vary," and "Results are not typical." Without a lot of work the results do vary—they vary from bad to worse. And the results are not typical because you typically can't get something for nothing.

Why do we expect it to be any different in God's economy? We can't expect blessings to fall from the sky just because we want them to. God blesses those who are willing to partner with Him in wholehearted effort. God works, and we work. God works as we work. I am acutely aware of this as I write this book. I am praying for God to help me. I want God to bless this book. But I still have to finish it. I can't expect God to bless an unwritten book. So, I work, and I write.

We can pray all day for blessing, but if we are not willing to exert our energy, we will be disappointed. A student can pray, "God give me an A on this test!" God will whisper back, "Have you studied?" A church can pray, "Lord, save people and grow our congregation." God will respond, "Are you willing to train, work together, give, and go witness to a lost world? Do that, and then I will bless your church." A businessman can pray, "Lord, bless this business," and God says, "Get up early, pray for wisdom, get busy, go after it, follow biblical principles, put Me first, and see what I'll do for you." To all of us, God says, "Pray, do your best, and watch Me work." If we fall, we must get back up. If we go left, we must get right. If we fail, we must return to this essential principle: God only establishes obedience and effort.

Certainly, our work alone is not sufficient for true success. The psalmist aptly states in Psalm 127:1, "Except the LORD build the house, they labour in vain that build it...." This statement is applicable to all human endeavors. Unless God is partnering with us in what we do, what we are doing will be ultimately empty of any eternal benefit. The verse could just as well read, "Except the Lord raise the family...," "Except the Lord builds the business...," "Except the Lord builds the church...," "Except the Lord...."

Psalm 127 was written "for Solomon." Solomon was a builder. He was a worker. Yet these words were a reminder to him that only God can establish our work. Verse 2 of the psalm says, "It is vain for you to rise up early, to sit up late, to eat the bread of sorrows: for so he giveth his beloved sleep." This is so profound! God is saying that He gives sleep to those who do not carry the burden of their labor alone. He is saying that there is a rest that comes in doing our best, living within reasonable limits, and trusting God for the results.

In the New Testament, Jesus says, "Come unto me, all ye that labour and are heavy laden, and I will give you rest. Take my yoke upon you, and learn of me; for I am meek and lowly in heart: and ye shall find rest unto your souls. For my yoke is easy, and my burden is light" (Matthew 11:28–30). His yoke is easy and His burden is light only because He enters the yoke with us to pull the weight and make it move. All becomes easier when we are working with God.

It's too bad that the nation of Israel did not understand this truth when they first had opportunity to enter the Promised Land. Sure, there were giants in the land. Sure, there were great walled cities full of seasoned fighters with which to deal. But God promised to work with His people and fight the battles for them. God promised to bless their effort and help them to stake their place in the Land of Promise. Instead of taking God up on His word, they turned back in fear. How sad.

The Israelites missed their opportunity. They lost the ideal. The prime time passed never to return. It was too late to enter Canaan, but it was not too late to learn the lesson of working with God.

Moses was now praying that God would use him to lead this same people for productive work and preparation for the future so the younger generation would be able to proceed with confidence. Moses believed that if the people could just see God's work and glory again, it would be enough to prompt them to believe in good things yet to come.

When Joshua finally led the nation of Israel into the land of Canaan, he was reminded by God that he should not depart from the Law, to meditate on it day and night, and "…to do according to all that is written therein…." Only then did God say, "…thou shalt make thy way prosperous and…have good success" (Joshua 1:8). This precept is something Joshua already knew; it was a lesson he had learned from Moses (Joshua 1:7). I propose that Joshua might not have been the leader he was designed to be had he not seen in his mentor the determination to stay true to God in his final years in the desert. Moses stayed faithful to the end, and God established his work, in part, by helping Joshua to succeed.

Moses' life ended with faith knowing that his work would be rewarded. He was leaving a legacy. At the end of his life, he spoke with confidence to the people telling them of how God would give them the land of Canaan. He blessed each tribe. He ordained Joshua to take his place. In his last days, God led him up to a high mountain to give him a glimpse of Canaan. He saw it from one end to the other. By faith, he pictured the plains of Palestine, full of people—his people. He died there on the mountaintop. (For the full story, read Deuteronomy 32–34.)

Moses died a fulfilled man, having seen with his own eyes the fruit of his labor. The people would possess the land, and they did for centuries. They possess part of it today. They will possess it fully in the future.

You and I can take part in this amazing legacy as we read the accounts and look forward to the full fruition of all that was promised. We read this psalm and prayer, written by Moses. We pray in kind and are encouraged to stay true to God no matter what happens on our journey of faith. The grace of God in the life of Moses is still bearing fruit today. I would call that an established work!

EXTRA POINTS TO PONDER

Questions

1. Can a person work for their salvation from sin's penalty (Ephesians 2:8–9)?

2. What are we to do after we are saved (Ephesians 2:10, Philippians 2:12)? What does this mean?

3. How does God work in our work (Philippians 2:13)?

4. If we abide in Christ, what can we expect (John 15:4–5)?

5. When God produces fruit through us, what is the result of that fruit (John 15:16)?

6. What is assured of concerning God's work in our lives according to Philippians 1:6?

Thought

As Christians, we have the privilege of engaging in a partnership with God. We are working together with Him. With that in mind, we can have confidence that if we abound in His work, our labors are not in vain (1 Corinthians 15:58). God will establish our work. If we commit our way to Him, He will bring it to pass (Psalm 37:5). So, no matter what has happened in our lives, "…let us not be weary in well doing: for in due season we shall reap, if we faint not" (Galatians 6:9).

CONCLUSION

So, what do we do when our lives turn in an unexpected direction? What do we do when we know that we've missed the mark of God's perfect will for the moment? When things will no longer be what they could have been—when Canaan is lost for good—we shouldn't sulk, quit, or throw a fit. We should pray. We should follow the pattern of Psalm 90 and pray the "Plan B" prayer.

Looking at this psalm of Moses we have learned that the "Plan B" prayer is a prayer of acceptance for an alternative way.

It is a prayer of worship acknowledging God's presence and drawing close to Him.

It is a prayer of urgency knowing that life is short and there is still much to do in the will of God.

It is a prayer for wisdom asking God to give understanding for how to go forward with purpose.

It is a prayer for mercy beseeching Him to diminish the consequences of sin and believing that He will still bless.

The "Plan B" prayer is a prayer of purpose. Where there's life, there's hope that God will establish our faithful effort.

This life is a life of frustration and failure. Denying this fact is to live with false optimism or in a state of denial. We don't want to live that way. Dwelling on the nature of life may lead us to utter despair. We don't want to do that either. We just need to be realistic. We are living between the days of "paradise lost" and "paradise regained." We are not in Heaven yet. We are going to have "desert experiences" due to sin in general, sin of our own, and the sins of others. Because of this, we have to learn to rely on God. We have to learn how to live in this lost world. We have to learn to find purpose in that which is less than perfect.

The message of Psalm 90 is both sour and sweet. It lends to a balanced and healthy view of life. It helps us to deal with reality—not with a sinful complacency, but with anticipation of God's prevailing grace. He will lead us forward.

We would be wise to go back to these verses often. We would be wise to study this psalm again and again. When we do, a prayer will proceed from our lips. It will be a passionate and positive prayer. God will answer that prayer. He will make a way for us. He will shine His light and illuminate the darkness. In God's light, we will be able to take the next step with confidence. We will look at the challenges and tasks ahead with courage. We will look up to Him and say, "Let's do this!"

ACKNOWLEDGMENTS

I thank my brother, Dan Zacharias, and my father-in-law, Mike Ashmore, for their help in editing the content found in this book. Dan has been an educator for over twenty-five years and now directs the Old Dominion Association of Christian Schools in Virginia. His expertise was invaluable. My father-in-law is a retired Air Force Lieutenant Colonel. For years, he served as an Operations Manager in the Pentagon—a job that required precise writing skills. He spent many hours reviewing and editing this book for me. Without his help, this book would have never gone to print.

Thank you both.

ABOUT THE AUTHOR

Dr. Tim Zacharias is a husband and father of four children. He is the founding pastor of the Community Baptist Church of Branford, Connecticut. Tim is also a trained counselor, conference speaker, and lecturer. He has taught in many settings including the Yale Law School where he directed a course on the Christian principles of early American law.

Visit us online

strivingtogether.com

wcbc.edu

Also available from

Striving Together Publications

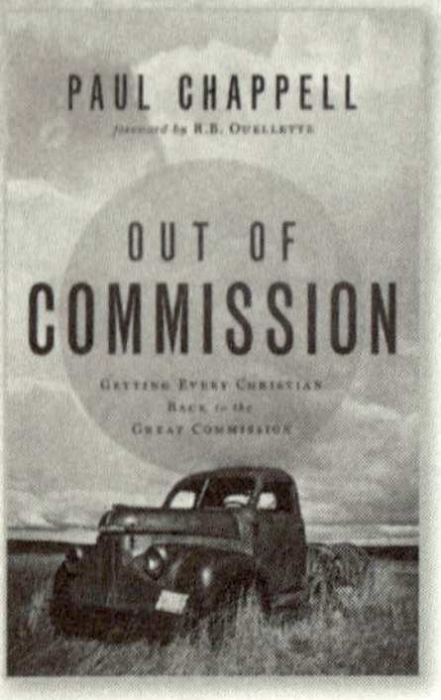

Out of Commission

Written for every Christian who desires to obey the Great Commission of Christ, this comprehensive volume is motivational and practical, diagnostic and corrective. Whether you are new to evangelism or an experienced soulwinner, *Out of Commission* will challenge and equip you to share your faith and more effectively reach your community for Christ. (256 pages, hardback)

Stewarding Life

This book will take you on a personal stewardship journey, equipping you to live effectively and biblically. It will challenge and equip you to strategically invest your most valuable resources for God's eternal purposes. Through these pages, discover God's most important principles for managing His most valuable gifts. (280 pages, hardback)

Living Beyond Your Capacity

The wonderful Holy Spirit of God desires to come into your life at salvation and unfold a daily work of power, grace, and transformation. He can enable you to live a supernatural life—a life that exceeds your human capacity. You can begin discovering and experiencing the Spirit-filled life today! (208 pages, paperback)

strivingtogether.com

Also available from

Striving Together Publications

Stewarding Life

Sunday School Curriculum

Stewarding life begins with a recognition that life itself is a gift from God and that He has provided every resource we need to carry out His purposes. In this thirteen-lesson series, you will discover God's most important principles for managing His most valuable gifts.

Abiding in Christ

Sunday School Curriculum

This unique study of John 15 takes you on a journey of learning how to become more like Christ by abiding in Him on a daily basis.

Real Church

Sunday School Curriculum

In this thirteen-lesson curriculum, discover authentic church life from the dynamic first century churches in the New Testament. Discover how you fit into God's eternal plan for changing the world through your local church.

strivingtogether.com